CBT *for*
PSYCHOTHERAPISTS

CBT *for* PSYCHOTHERAPISTS

THEORY AND PRACTICE

AVIGDOR BONCHEK

PARTRIDGE

To order additional copies of this book, contact
Toll Free 800 101 2657 (Singapore)
Toll Free 1 800 81 7340 (Malaysia)
orders.singapore@partridgepublishing.com

www.partridgepublishing.com/singapore

Contents

Preface

The goal of this book is to give students and practicing psychologists a basic understanding of the theory behind cognitive behavioural therapy (CBT) and a view of treatment programs that derive from the theory to deal with a variety of psychological problems. It also encourages readers and practitioners of CBT to think critically, to think outside the box. All that is claimed to be CBT isn't necessarily the best of CBT. The book is based on the professional literature on this subject, but I do occasionally offer ideas based on my own experience.

Chapter 1

What Is CBT?

"CBT" stands for cognitive behavioural therapy. In the realm of psychotherapy, there are hundreds of different therapeutic approaches. But there are two main approaches: dynamic and behavioural. The dynamic approaches are based on Freud's psychoanalytic theory; the behavioural approaches (including CBT) are based on learning theory.

How CBT Differs

I will cite a case that came to me recently in order to exemplify the difference between the CBT-oriented and dynamic-oriented therapies.

A middle-aged woman, married with seven children, came down with a crippling disease. She was confined to a wheelchair and could not take care of her household duties. She hired a woman to cook and clean for her. Five of her children were married and out of the house. Just a seventeen-year-old girl and a twelve-year-old boy remained at home.

The problem was that the daughter refused to have anything to do with the helper. She wouldn't eat the food she prepared or let her clean her room. The girl refused to touch anything this woman touched. If she opened the refrigerator, the girl would only open the door holding a towel. This caused much anger and discomfort for the mother and the family.

The girl agreed to go to therapy and was seen by a dynamic-oriented therapist. The mother understood from the therapist the goal of therapy. The therapist explained that she understood the girl's behaviour as indirect anger towards the mother. Because the mother no longer functioned like a mother, the girl saw this as a rejection of her as her daughter. By ignoring and banning the helper, the girl was getting back at her mother through the mother's substitute.

The therapist then instructed the mother to go out of her way to show her love and caring for her daughter. She should not be angry with her – just the opposite. She should understand what is happening emotionally to the daughter and try to overcome it by warmth and love, without criticism.

After several months of therapy, there was little change in the girl's behaviour; the therapist thought maybe medication should be used.

The mother then turned to me and a CBT approach.

I explained how I saw it. I said, "The girl may be angry, but that does not justify her behaviour." I suggested the following steps:

1) The girl should not derive any benefit from her behaviour. For example, she had made a deal with her brother for him to help her clean up her room, and she would repay him with another favour. I said this should be stopped. If the helper couldn't clean her room, then the girl must do it herself. No one should make food for her if she refused to eat the helper's food.

2) There should be no accommodation to the girl's whims.

must respond to his crying in a different way. This different way is in the present; we change the reaction to his fear in the present, because his fear is in the present as well.

2) **Individualised treatment plan for each patient**. There is no "one size fits all." The problem is analysed, and the treatment is made to fit this problem with this person in this situation.

3) **Clear operational – behavioural – goals for each patient**. "Feeling better," while a good achievement, is not behavioural. It is hard if not impossible to measure, so it is not a useful goal for therapy. Nor is "insight" a useful goal. The bottom line in CBT is helping people overcome their problems, which the dynamic approach calls "symptoms."

We strive for symptom relief and are not embarrassed by it, because once it is truly achieved, patients can go on with their lives.

4) **The active, directing therapist**. Therapists want to move their patients forward. They direct the therapy; they assign homework and coach their patients. In any event, all therapists are directive, even dynamic ones. It is impossible not to be directive and influence the client. Even dynamic therapists decide which of their patient's words they will comment on. This is directing in an indirect way. Ironically, the more therapists try to be neutral, the more they are influential because the patient searches all the harder to discern what the therapist thinks.

5) **Normalcy versus pathology**. CBT therapists usually see their patients as having a problem rather than seeing them as problem patients. We would say dynamic therapy sees the patient as the problem, while CBT sees the problem as the problem.

WHEN THE PATIENT IS THE PROBLEM

WHEN THE PROBLEM IS THE PATIENT

The Therapist as Researcher

There is another unique aspect of the CBT therapist/patient relationship that should be mentioned. Since all treatment includes continuous measurement of the target behaviour, therapists are also researchers. Their research has but one subject (the patient), but they compare the patient's progressive behaviour change with pretreatment behaviour. This is essential for treatment and provides therapists with a real-life experiment: testing their treatment's effectiveness.

Thinking Outside the Box

CBT theory is clear and straightforward. For that reason, it is relatively easy to learn. That advantage is also a disadvantage. Therapists may fall into the trap of "easy understanding." By that, I mean they relate to the theory and its applications – particularly those that are accepted by the CBT community – with little critical thought. That is never good.

The present-day CBT situation is not perfect. It should be obvious to say that we will learn new applications in the future. When therapists are confronted by a problem in their therapy, they search the professional literature to see what others have found. This is a wise approach, but it is not sufficient. They should think through their dilemma and see if, based on CBT theory, they can come up with something new. That's how our body of knowledge constantly grows. It is for this reason that I think all therapists should be critical of applications that may not be perfect and think outside the box to come up with new applications.

In this book, you will find examples of this.

Chapter 2

Basic Nonspecific Factors in Psychotherapy

Before we get into the essence of CBT treatment, we should first mention those factors in therapy that are important for success in *any* form of psychotherapy and in CBT as well.

These factors are elements in the therapist's personality. They are not techniques, though they can be learned by the therapist.

These factors enhance success in therapy because they build the confidence of patients in their therapists. This is essential for all any type of psychotherapy to succeed.

Back in the 1950s, Dr Carl Rogers pinpointed the following three factors that are essential to success in psychotherapy:

- empathy
- genuineness
- positive regard

Empathy (Validating the Patient's Experience)

Empathy is showing patients you understand what they are feeling – not just thinking. That is, to validate their feelings in a nonjudgmental way means implying and conveying that what they feel is perfectly okay. It is not a sign that they are crazy, as they may have feared, or that they are self-pitying. Empathy does not mean you agree with them, only that you understand what they feel. This is a crucial element of gaining the patient's cooperation. That cooperation is very important in CBT, more important than it is in other types of therapy, because CBT always encourages patients to do homework between sessions. Without their cooperation and motivation, the chances of them doing the homework when they are not in the presence of the therapist is greatly reduced. So cooperation is the first stage of treatment; without it, therapy will fail. It deserves the same amount of effort and time as the actual treatment itself. Empathy shows patients that you are listening to them and that you understand their pain. For that reason, any hint of criticism is out of place. Criticism can take the form of belittling the seriousness of the problem. It can take the form of expecting them to "stop complaining" and start working on their problems. If they feel criticised, they will clam up and stop being open for fear of criticism. We need them to be open to best understand what exactly bothers them and why. Knowing this points us in the right direction to focus our therapeutic procedures. Some techniques for empathy are just to repeat the last words the patient said as a question.

For example, she said, "My mother always nags me."

Therapist: "Your mother always nags you?"

This keeps the discussion going and encourages her to elaborate on her statement. An additional way to achieve empathy is to summarise the patient's words either at the end of the session or after a long comment of hers. If the summary is correct, the patient will show her agreement. If it is not correct, she will correct the therapist's summary, and the therapist will thereby gain a better understanding of the patient's situation.

Genuineness

Genuineness means therapists realise they are human, just as the patient is. Therapists may not suffer from what the patient does, but that does not make them super human. There should be no looking down at the patient. This genuineness avoids hypocrisy. For example, if we expect the patient to come to the sessions on time, therapists must also come on time. If they are late, they don't pass over it silently; they apologise, as they would expect the patient to do.

Genuineness includes looking at patients when talking to them.

The therapist's behaviour during the session conveys either genuineness or superiority. The therapeutic relationship is a partnership, and therapists create that partnership by their behaviour towards the patient.

Spontaneity is an important indication of the therapist's genuineness. By responding in a straightforward manner, patients feel you're with them. Long silences before a response conveys an unnatural conversation (they may think, *I must first be careful with what I say*). On the other hand, patients usually see spontaneous messages as genuine.

Positive Regard

Positive regard means simply that you have a positive feeling towards patients. As we said, you don't look down at them as "poor souls." If I appreciate a patient's sense of humour, I will tell her so. I often say, "I don't treat problems. I treat people." By that I mean if I treat a single woman and I know she hopes someday to be able to get married, I tell her that I see my work continuing (though not necessarily through continuous sessions) until she settles down in married life. I convey that I believe she is capable of a normal life, and our work consists of helping her get there.

Having a nonjudgmental attitude towards the thoughts, feelings, and actions of the patient is essential. Warmth is central to the patient/ client relationship. Warmth is conveyed in many ways: tone of voice, facial expression, and of course what we say. Such things cannot be faked; they must be genuine.

Active Listening

Active listening is a powerful tool for therapists. Actually, it is a powerful tool for all kinds of communication, professional or otherwise. It is central to all therapy. It means that listening is a behaviour that involves the therapist's activity. Active listening has three main elements.

(1) **Clarification:** This can be done by repeating the patient's words as a question. We mentioned this above as part of empathy. Therapists summarise their comments with a slight twist – to point out the essence of the comment, usually by adding an emotional component in the summary.

> **Patient:** I just feel hopeless.
> **Therapist:** Tell me more about what you mean.
> **Patient:** I mean there is no hope for me. I will be single till I die.
> **Therapist:** What do you mean? Have you given up on meeting new men?
> **Patient:** I don't see any chance of me getting married anymore.
> **Therapist:** Do you mean you are giving up on meeting new men? Or are you referring to something different, like giving up on life and possibly harming yourself?
> **Patient:** I am not referring to suicide, if that is what you mean, but I am feeling really depressed. Each day seems like such a struggle, and I often just feel like staying in bed. When I said "give up," I guess I was referring to not wanting to face all the struggles I face in life: my school work, financial problems, relationship problems, etc.

Notice that the clarifying statement and question helped the therapist and patient to more fully explore her feelings and thoughts. Given this new information, the therapist is in a better position to explore in more detail the patient's concerns and to set up targeted efforts and strategies for treatment.

(2) **Paraphrasing:** This means restating the patient's main thoughts in a slightly different way.

(3) **Reflection:** This means reflecting back the emotions the patient is experiencing. This gives therapists the chance to see if they correctly understand the patient's emotional state. Below is an example of reflection through paraphrasing:

Patient: Today at work, my boss really insulted me. Every day is a struggle with him. I don't really know if I can take much more of this. The pain is too much.
Therapist: Your emotional struggle is getting you down. It is so painful you don't know how much longer you can take it.
Patient: Yes, that is how I feel. But leaving and looking for another job is also frightening.
Therapist: It seems you feel trapped.
Patient: Exactly. I don't know where to turn from here. It's not that I think I can't do this work well; I *know* I can. It's that I can't handle criticism; I don't know how to respond to it.

In this example of paraphrasing, the therapist gives back to the patient what he heard, which allows the patient to hear her own words and react with a more detailed response. The use of paraphrasing in this example facilitated a deeper understanding of the issue but also conveyed to the patient a feeling of being heard and understood.

Setting the Stage for Beginning

Once we have achieved the patient's confidence and willingness to actively deal with his problems, we must be sure not to fall into common traps that can ensnare therapists and retard therapeutic progress. One common error is to try to relieve his anxiety by facile comments of reassurance. This is an error because reassurance relieves anxiety only momentarily but not in the long run. If the patient feels he is being listened to and understood, he will have the patience and fortitude to tolerate his anxiety until real corrective techniques can be applied.

When patients have several problems or several different manifestations of one problem, therapists must choose which one they will tackle first; it is best to hear patients out and see which one they prefer to work on first. This enables us to use their motivation, which is crucial, in working on the problem. The only exception to this is when patients choose a problem which the therapist believes may be too difficult for them to succeed at, at this point. Then we must assure them that we will deal with that problem, but not right now; we must prepare the way by working on lesser problems first.

Once the goals are agreed upon, therapeutic work can begin. We again stress that the above nonspecific factors of the therapist's approach are crucial to success. This is even more true for CBT than for the talk therapies (i.e., dynamic therapies). We can call CBT a "doing therapy," because we ask patients to do things (meet their challenges) between sessions. And only with complete confidence and a positive feeling towards the therapist will the patient be willing to put out the effort needed to meet these challenges.

Let us now begin with the theoretical basis for CBT.

Chapter 3

Operant and Classical Conditioning

Kurt Lewin, a famous research psychologist of the past century, said, "There is nothing more practical than a good theory."

The statement sounds counterintuitive, because we usually think of theory as "theoretical," meaning distanced somewhat from what happens in reality. But his point was that a *good* theory by definition is closely bound to reality.

This is precisely the situation with the theory behind CBT.

The theory forms the underpinning of various treatment techniques, as we will see when we discuss CBT techniques.

The theory behind CBT is B.F. Skinner's theories of learning. The laws of learning are important because behaviourists assume that all behaviour – normal and abnormal – is learned. And they are learned according to the laws of learning. Skinner's theory was experimentally tested in thousands of cases with animals. Later, it was found that they apply equally well to human behaviour.

Below is a discussion of this theory.

Behaviour is looked at in the context of before and after it occurs.

$$A \rightarrow B \rightarrow C$$
A = antecedent conditions, B = behaviour, and C = consequences

This means that in any given situation, a person's behaviour always takes place in time between what happened before (A) and what happens afterwards (C). This is quite obvious, but its implications are not so obvious.

Keeping the above formula in mind, we can differentiate two different kinds of learning:

Classical Learning

Classical learning is based on the A→B part of the formula. That means that when a certain behaviour is paired with and follows a certain event (sound, smell, or whatever), if this is repeated several times, then eventually the event itself will elicit the behaviour.

The famous experiments of Ivan Pavlov, at the beginning of the twentieth century, are the prime example of this. Pavlov, who studied the physiological aspects of dogs salivating, found to his surprise that when he brought the dogs their lunch, they had already begun salivating before he even entered the room with the food. Dogs, like humans, salivate when they have food in their mouth. But he wondered, how would they know they were getting food? Then he realised that they heard his footsteps in the corridor, and this sound was the "A" in the formula. Whenever A (sound of walking) came, salivation (B) began because in the past, the sound of footsteps in the corridor was paired with receiving food.

That is classical conditioning. Pavlov went on to experiment by pairing eating with the sound of a tuning fork. Remarkably, he found that the amount of salivation from the dogs depended on how similar the decibel sound of the tuning fork was to the original sound of the fork they heard when it was first paired with food. The closer the decibel sound was to the original one, the more saliva was elicited; the further from the original, the less saliva. This was truly a law of behaviour, similar in reliability to the law of gravity.

Classical learning of behaviour is usually relevant to teaching *automated* responses like salivating. The dogs don't control their salivation; it is an instinctual behaviour.

This is not too important for psychotherapists; they rarely deal with salivation. But it is very relevant to other automatic human responses, the most significant being fear and anxiety. Fear and anxiety, as all who have experienced them knows, come on involuntarily. Because they are controlled by Pavlov's laws of classical conditioning, we have a way to treat anxiety and fear. We will address this later when we discuss techniques for anxiety in therapy.

Operant Learning

The second type of learning is operant conditioning. This is based on the other part of the formula above: B→C. Here we mean that behaviour is learned by what happens *after* the behaviour occurs. The consequences that come after a behaviour determine if and when the behaviour will occur again, and if it will increase in the future or decrease. When we think of problematic behaviour, this is quite significant. We may have here the treatment answer to all therapeutic problems. But while there is much truth in that, in the final analysis, the picture is usually more complicated.

There are three possible consequences to any behaviour:

The possible consequences are that something good happened or something bad happened or nothing happened.

When something good happens, it is called **reinforcement.**

When something bad happens, it is called **punishment.**

When nothing happens, it is called **extinction**.

These terms have to be explained.

Reinforcement is anything that happens after a behaviour and that behaviour occurs more frequently in the future. We define it this way, by its effects, because we can't say simply "something good," since each person has different likes and dislikes, so what is good for one may not be good for the other.

Of course, there are certain things we assume people like: money, compliments, or other goodies. But this is always just an assumption. So if we have a plan and use a certain reinforcement that we thought would be good but it does not increase the behaviour we are reinforcing, we must determine if the reinforcement is not positive in the person's mind. If it isn't, it is not a reinforcement.

Here is a good example of this. A third grade teacher found that three children always came late to class in the morning: two boys and a girl. She made a rule: "Anyone who comes late will have to stay after school for as many minutes as they were late; if they are fifteen minutes late, then they stay fifteen minutes after school before they go home." The next day, all three were late again, so the teacher announced that the boy who came ten minutes late would stay ten minutes after school is over. The boy who was a half-hour late would stay a half-hour after school, and the girl, who was fifteen minutes late, would stay fifteen minutes. The following day, the two boys came on time, but the girl was late again, so she stayed after school again. This continued to happen for a whole week. The teacher finally took the girl aside and asked why she continued to be late, even though she was kept after school. The girl explained, "My mother works, and my older sister comes home much later from school, so I actually prefer to stay here with you instead of going to an empty home."

So the teacher changed the rule for this girl. "When you come on time, you can stay an hour with me after school, but if you come late to school, you go home with everyone else." From then on, the girl came on time.

In short, what was a punishment for the boys was a reward for the girl. So if our original plan is not successful, we have to check if our assumption about what is a reinforcement and what is a punishment is correct for this person.

Punishment is something "bad" (unwanted) by the person.

It can be something negative, like being hit, or something negative in the sense that an expected good does not happen. A student may not be allowed to go on a class trip.

Behaviour which has a negative consequence (i.e., punishment) will decrease in frequency over time, and eventually it will stop completely.

Extinction: When nothing of significance happens after the behaviour. In cases of human behaviour, this usually means that people in the environment ignore – do not respond – to the behaviour. When this happens consistently, the behaviour eventually dies out. We must caution that when extinction is used, the immediate reaction is that the negative behaviour increases (to seek out the attention which he didn't get). But if the behaviour continues to be ignored, it will drop out.

Types of Reinforcers

There are several types of reinforcers, each with its own pluses and minuses:

1) **Material reinforcers**. This is something like a book, a piece of candy, a pen, and so on. These concrete reinforcers are helpful to begin a program because they are very much wanted. But they must be phased out because in the real world, people don't get such rewards for every good act they do.

2) **Social reinforcers**. This means a smile, a compliment, or other recognition for good behaviour. It is inexpensive (!) and very powerful. It is also similar to what happens in the real world. So even if material reinforcers are used in the beginning of treatment, they should always be paired with verbal praise. That praise itself can eventually be used alone.

3) **Tokens**. These are symbolic reinforcements like money. They have no intrinsic value except the value we give them. For example, if we give out points for good behaviour, we can say ten points equals a book or a pen or whatever. We determine its value. Its advantage is that we can break down tasks to smaller pieces and give a point for each piece, even if the complete behaviour is not done. The most obvious example is a school test, with ten questions. We give each question a point value. This is also useful in teaching complex behaviours; we give each part of the behaviour separate point value, so we don't create an all-or-nothing situation, which would be the case if we only reinforced a complete act. Points are also good because they connect today's behaviour with tomorrow's behaviour. The person is marching towards a goal in the future; this strengthens motivation. On the other hand, for example, a smile today may or may not influence me tomorrow.

4) **Other behaviour**. We can use behaviour itself as reinforcement for other behaviour. A preferred behaviour can be used to reinforce a less preferred behaviour. The simplest example is to tell your child, "First, do your homework (behaviour 1) then you can go out to play (behaviour 2)". This looks simple-minded, but when used wisely, it can have some surprising results. We will give examples of this further on.

Types of Punishments

- **physical:** hitting, lashes, and so on
- **social:** insulting or embarrassing the person publicly
- **response cost** (fines)
- **time-out**

Both physical and social punishments should never be used. They cause more problems than they could possibly solve, but the following are the two that can be used:

Response cost also means fines. These can be either actual monetary fines or point fines, if a token program is used. In all cases, the rules for losing money (or points) must be clearly spelled out. There should also be a way to earn back lost points.

Time-out means having the child taken out of the social setting (e.g., the classroom) and placed in a guarded place with no social interaction. Time-out should be short: five or ten minutes at the most. After this, the child is returned to class. If he again disrupts, he is immediately taken back to time-out. He should not be sent to time-out without an adult taking him, to make sure he gets there. He is taken without being lectured, quietly, and respectfully.

Increasing the Influence of the Consequences

The above-mentioned consequences influence behaviour in a natural way. But their influence can be made stronger when these three rules are followed:

1) **Immediacy:** The sooner a consequence follows the behaviour, the stronger and surer will be its effect. Giving a reward within minutes (or seconds) of the behaviour is much more influential than giving it a half-hour later.

   In fact, a half-hour later, the reward may have no effect at all.

2) **Consistency:** The consequence must be given in a consistent way, not sometimes yes and sometimes no. Inconsistent application of a consequence will have only a weak effect (if at all) on the behaviour.

   Consistency is particularly crucial in early stages of changing behaviour; once the new behaviour has begun to be established, we can be somewhat less careful about consistency.

3) **Timing:** How often and when reinforcement is given also influences the behaviour. By this, I mean he can receive reinforcement every time the behaviour occurs, or it can be given every second or third time it occurs. Skinner called this the schedule of reinforcement. It is the ratio between behaviour and receiving a reinforcement; ratios include 1:1 (every time), 1:2 (every second time), 1:3 (every third time), and so on. Different ratios have different effects on behaviour. The rule is that to begin changing behaviour, we use 1:1 and then move to 1:2 and so forth. This is important because when we want to *begin* change and ensure there is change, we reinforce frequently (1:1). But life outside the clinic or the school is not so kind. So to prepare the person for real life while guaranteeing that

new behaviour is quickly learned and is not extinguished by too little reinforcement, we strengthen the behaviour gradually. Skinner did some studies where he reinforced pigeons to peck at a certain button up to 20,000 times before getting even slight reinforcement. That's a bit too much for our purposes, but it shows what is possible.

Here is an illustrative parable regards a man who saw another man lift a grown bull. The first asked the second how he was capable of lifting such a heavy animal. The second replied, "When this bull was born, it was a small calf. So I lifted it up every day; after it got larger, I continued to lift it up. As the calf grew into a heavy bull, so too my muscles grew to enable me to lift him."

This is the effect of gradually spacing out the reinforcement; eventually, one does the same thing for less reinforcement.

There are two types of schedules. One is based on the ratio of behaviour done to receiving a reinforcement, as we mentioned above. The other depends on time. That means the person will receive reinforce only if a certain amount of time has passed since the last reinforcement. This causes the behaviour to increase when the new time arrives.

An example of this is when a person is expecting an important letter. Since the mailman only comes between 10 and 11 a.m., he will check his mailbox more often as this time approaches. After 12 noon, he will no longer check until the next day. So we can predict and control behaviour knowing this. Another well-known example of a time-controlled schedule is when students study for tests. If they know the next test is on March 15, they will study very few hours in January, if at all; only as March 15 approaches will their study time spike. And certainly after the test, they will spend no more time studying.

A teacher who knows this may switch to giving tests at unannounced times, say once every three weeks; this keeps students always in a study mode.

A personal experience of mine showed me how this can affect everyday life. When we first got married, my landlady came to visit my wife. She came at 11 a.m. and saw my wife ironing my shirts. Then and there, she taught the young bride a lesson: "Let me give you some advice," she said. "If you do the housework now, what do you do in the afternoon?" "Oh," my wife answered, "I read a book or a magazine, just relax." "But then your husband comes home and sees you doing nothing." My landlady advised my wife, "Best to do your reading in the morning and start your housework before he comes home from work. Then he'll see you working and appreciate you."

Chapter 4

From Theory to Practice: Therapeutic Applications

Until now, we have been talking about consequences as laws of nature. They weren't *invented* by Pavlov and Skinner; they were *discovered* by them. These behaviour changes happen naturally, without psychologists treating anyone. If we leave the house without a coat and find it's raining, we naturally go back to get a coat or umbrella to avoid the punishment of the rain. When a baby holds his milk bottle, he instinctively bends it to the right angle so he gets the milk to the nipple of the bottle; when there is less milk in the bottle, he holds it at a new angle in order to continue to get his reinforcement. No one taught him this; it comes naturally.

But as CBT therapists move from theory to practice, they try to make wise use of these laws of behaviour to help accomplish their therapeutic goals.

Let us see how this is done. We will start with conquering fear, because this was one the first therapeutic applications of the laws of learning back in the 1950s.

Phobias

When a patient came with a phobia – an irrational fear of a harmless object or situation   Dr Joseph Wolpe of Temple University in Philadelphia used what he called systematic desensitisation.

Some Background

As background to Wolpe's technique, we must be aware of an experiment which was done nearly a hundred years ago.

A ten-month-old baby was given a peaceful rabbit to play with. After several times when he enjoyed touching the rabbit, then every time the child touched the rabbit, the experimenter stood at a distance and made a sudden, loud, frightening noise. The child was startled by the noise. After pairing the noise and touching the rabbit several times, the baby became afraid of the rabbit; he cried and crawled away from it when he saw it. This new fear was taught by means of Pavlovian conditioning: pairing behaviour (seeing the rabbit) with another event (the loud noise). Eventually, the event (loud noise = fear) was attached to the peaceful rabbit in the child's mind.

Then another experiment was done to try to extinguish the child's fear. A young child who feared rabbits was seated in a high chair in a room where the door was open into the second room. In this second room was a rabbit sitting peacefully eating a carrot; the child could see the rabbit from her chair; at this distance, it didn't evoke crying from her. They gave her ice cream to eat while the door was open and she could see the rabbit.

Now a pleasant experience was paired with seeing the rabbit (also a Pavlovian-type pairing). Step-by-step, the baby was brought closer to the rabbit, each time while enjoying her ice cream. Soon, she was very close while still in her high chair, then she was put on the floor (also enjoying ice cream) with the rabbit nearby. Now, she no longer feared the rabbit. Her fear had been overcome (or we could say had been unlearned).

This was the treatment for overcoming fear. Of course, adults would have to be dealt with differently. Here is where Wolpe and his systematic desensitisation comes in.

Systematic Desensitisation

Systematic desensitisation consists of two parts:

1) Learning deep muscle relaxation (DMR)
2) Pairing the relaxed state with a mental image of an ascending hierarchy of feared situations

Deep Muscle Relaxation

You learn DMR by sitting in a quiet place where there will be no outside disturbances for fifteen to twenty minutes. You tighten (flex) the muscles of your right arm and then relax them, all the time paying close attention to how these muscles feel, particularly when they become relaxed. You go through your whole body this way: left arm, right foot, left foot, chest muscles, neck muscles, face muscles, and so on. The whole procedure could take fifteen to twenty minutes. If you can record the directions on a tape, you can then listen to the recording as you go through the procedure.

By doing this five times, you should be able to reach a good level of relaxation.

Hierarchy of Feared Situations

You then write out all the various situations concerning a particular fear and then order them from least feared to most feared. For example, if you feared dogs, you would start your hierarchy at the bottom with walking on the street where there are no dogs. Then you see a dog on a leash two hundred feet ahead, then a hundred fifty feet ahead, then a hundred feet ahead, closer and closer all the time. You envision yourself passing the dog on a leash. It is most relevant that the dog should be barking as you go. After this, you introduce the dog at a distance with no leash, until the dog passes you while it is not on a leash.

The more items on the hierarchy, the more helpful it is.

You write these items on cards and order them with the least fearful on top. You then sit down to get into relaxation; when you are relaxed, you view and imagine the first scene (with your eyes closed). You continue to imagine it until you can imagine it with much less fear; you do it again until the fear is gone. Then you go on to the next card (slightly more feared).

Again, you imagine it, and again, you do it enough times to bring the fear down to your comfort zone. In any one session, you should try to do four or five different levels of fear.

When you reach the uppermost fear, you can venture outside to face a real situation. It would be best if you arrange that a friend with a dog on a leash come out to meet you. This will be your validation that you have overcome your fear. But full recovery only comes after many walks outside, exposing yourself to the possibility of seeing a dog.

This technique can be used for the fear of flying, for claustrophobia, or any other single fear. Complex fears have to be handled differently.

As we can see, this technique is derived directly from Pavlov's principle of classical conditioning. We see how the theory is very practical in this case.

There is another way to treat fears successfully; it is called exposure and response prevention.

Exposure and Response Prevention

This technique for dealing with the variety of anxiety disorders developed over the past thirty years. You expose yourself to your feared situation, meaning you meet your fear face-to-face. You face your fear and do not flee from it, this is the "response prevention" part. You prevent your usual response (behaviour) of fleeing your fear, by staying in the feared situation long enough to give your anxiety time to come down; it always comes down, eventually. Then you are in the feared situation with a positive consequence of feeling less fear. Your relief of fear is a reinforcement (a positive event) and that in turn reinforces your ability to meet your fear, which occurred right before your anxiety subsided. In addition, since right before the anxiety subsided, you had felt anxiety in the presence of the feared situation, this anxiety is also reduced. After several experiences like this, you can now meet the feared object without anxiety.

This explanation is based on operant conditioning, as we explained above. A behaviour (facing the fear) that is followed by a positive effect (reduced anxiety) will reoccur more often in the future.

We see that two different techniques based two different types of learning (operant and classical) may both be therapeutically helpful. There is a debate among clinicians about which method is better; some say both work equally well. I am of the belief that exposure is the better choice.

Let us continue with CBT treatment for anxiety disorders.

First Session

In the initial session, we must make sure we understand the problem we are to treat. We must understand it from the patient's perspective.

We begin by asking simply "How can I help you? What is the problem you want us to work on?"

To clarify things for myself, I often ask, "When you are no longer disturbed by your problem, how will your life be different? What will you be able to do that you can't do today?"

The last part is crucial. It gives the therapist some clear behavioural goals for therapy.

I also ask if she has ever succeeded in dealing with this problem, or any aspect of it, in the past. This offers me an opportunity to hear the patient's strengths so I can utilise them in the future. It is also an opportunity to compliment the patient on her achievement, which can strengthen her self-confidence in the coming work.

In order to understand the problem from the patient's viewpoint, we engage in **active listening,** as we discussed above. I will repeat here only the salient points: listening is ordinarily a passive act. He talks, we listen. But active listening means the listener (therapist) is active; she asks questions to clarify if she has understood correctly. She corrects her misunderstanding (if there was one) and sends that back to the patient to validate. She will also summarise in order to focus on what she thinks is essential and most important for the patient. Again, she asks the patient if her summary was correct. This is crucial for effective therapy. A patient will often drop out if he thinks the therapist doesn't *really* understand the depth and severity of his problem.

So even if we have seen hundreds of similar cases, we should investigate each case as if it is our first. This gives the patient the feeling that we are working to hear him out. And, in fact, we may actually see a new twist in this patient's unique pain.

We can also use brief questionnaires to help understand the patient's situation and worries. The Hamilton Anxiety Scale is a useful questionnaire.

Hamilton Anxiety Scale

Below is a list of phrases that describe certain feelings that people have. Rate the patients by finding the answer which best describes the extent to which they have these conditions. Select one of the five responses for each of the fourteen questions.

	Not Present	Mild	Moderate	Severe	Very Severe
1. Anxious Mood Worries, anticipation of the worst, fearful anticipation, irritability.	◌	◌	◌	◌	◌
2. Tension Feelings of tension, fatigability, startle response, moved to tears easily, trembling, feelings of restlessness, inability to relax.	◌	◌	◌	◌	◌
3. Fears Of dark, of strangers, of being left alone, of animals, of traffic, of crowds.	◌	◌	◌	◌	◌
4. Insomnia Difficulty in falling asleep, broken sleep, unsatisfying sleep and fatigue on waking, dreams, nightmares, night terrors.	◌	◌	◌	◌	◌

	Not Present	Mild	Moderate	Severe	Very Severe
5. Intellectual Difficulty in concentration, poor memory.	○	○	○	○	○
6. Depressed Mood Loss of interest, lack of pleasure in hobbies, depression, early waking, diurnal swing.	○	○	○	○	○
7. Somatic (muscular) Pains and aches, twitching, stiffness, myoclonic jerks, grinding of teeth, unsteady voice, increased muscular tone.	○	○	○	○	○
8. Somatic (sensory) Tinnitus, blurring of vision, hot and cold flushes, feelings of weakness, pricking sensation.	○	○	○	○	○
9. Cardiovascular Symptoms Tachycardia, palpitations, pain in chest, throbbing of vessels, fainting feelings, missing beat.	○	○	○	○	○
10. Respiratory Symptoms Pressure or constriction in chest, choking feelings, sighing, dyspnoea.	○	○	●	○	○

	Not Present	Mild	Moderate	Severe	Very Severe
11. Gastrointestinal Symptoms Difficulty in swallowing, wind, abdominal pain, burning sensations, abdominal fullness, nausea, vomiting, borborygmi, looseness of bowels, loss of weight, constipation.	○	○	○	○	○
12. Genitourinary Symptoms Frequency of micturition, urgency of micturition, amenorrhea, menorrhagia, development of rigidity, premature ejaculation, loss of libido, impotence.	○	○	○	○	○
13. Autonomic Symptoms Dry mouth, flushing, pallor, tendency to sweat, giddiness, tension headache, raising of hair.	○	○	○	○	○
14. Behaviour at Interview Fidgeting, restlessness or pacing, tremor of hands, furrowed brow, strained face, sighing or rapid respiration, facial pallor, swallowing, etc.	○	○	○	○	○

Score my Answers

Sum the scores from all fourteen parameters.

14–17 = Mild Anxiety
18–24 = Moderate Anxiety
25–30 = Severe Anxiety

What is good about this questionnaire is that each question has several levels (from none to severe). This means we can use it at the beginning and during the therapy to see if any gradual changes have occurred.

Formulating a Treatment Plan

After hearing the patient out, we try to formulate the outlines of a treatment plan. We can only do this with the cooperation and agreement of the patient. I would begin by asking her what she would like to work on first. If you think it is not too big a challenge to begin with, go with it. But if you fear she may not succeed at fulfilling the challenge, then I would explain that it might be too difficult and that we should leave it for later in the therapy. The *size* of the challenge is not crucial; the *success* of meeting whatever challenge is decided on is crucial. Success builds self-confidence and increases motivation for future work.

How Therapy Sessions Work

The therapist should, at the first session, explain the format and purpose of therapeutic sessions.

You should stress that the focus of every session is to hear how patients handled the challenge that was agreed upon in the previous session. You listen to their successes and failures, compliment them on their successes, and then with their input try to analyse why they failed (if they did). In addition to the central focus on symptom management, you tell patients that they are free to bring up any topic that is important to them. You don't limit them exclusively to the CBT goal of overcoming their problem. You allow them to use the session for any other matter that concerns them.

Beginning Work on Phobia Treatment

After you have heard the dimensions of their phobia and have a hierarchy of their levels of fear, you begin with the lowest level. I described above two different approaches to phobia treatment. One was systematic desensitisation by relaxation and guided imagery; the other was exposure and response prevention. I prefer to use both of these techniques to achieve maximum chance of success. I would first teach relaxation and then pair it with the fear situation lowest on the hierarchy. After two sessions of this, I would suggest going out into the field. CBT at its best sometimes requires you to leave your office in order to help the patient in the real-life exposure challenge.

Let us take as our example a phobia of snakes. A young woman I treated panicked by just seeing a snake on television. She would immediately cry out in shock and then leave the room and not return until she was sure there was no snake on the screen.

We found a university centre where snakes were kept in cages.

We went together to this place. It was a series of cabins; in each cabin were cages of different types of snakes. When we approached one of the cabins, I asked her how close she could come without feeling fear. She was assured that she that would not enter the cabin without her consent (a promise which must always be kept). We came up to the line in the sand, to where she said she could approach the cabin with little or no fear.

The next session, we did guided imagery. After having visited the scene with the snake cabins, she now could better imagine a specific challenge. At the same (longer) session, I asked if we could go again to the cabin with the snakes. Again, I assured her nothing would be done without her consent. We approached the cabin to the previous point, and I asked her if she would try to approach a few more steps, but not too close to cause panic. She consented and took four or five steps. I warmly congratulated her, and with that we ended the session.

The next session was similar: first guided imagery and then a trip to the snakes. This was a university student, and she said she could not afford all the sessions. I made a deal with her. Since she knew my format in the sessions, she could treat herself, each time getting closer and closer to the cabin and eventually entering it. She agreed and kept me informed by phone. Eventually, after several weeks, she was able to enter the cabin and touch a snake in the cage; eventually, she even picked up the snake. She took a photo (before the age of selfies) of that scene and sent it to me.

This is a dramatic example of how a motivated patient can learn the techniques of CBT and can treat herself and achieve complete success.

Below is the note she sent me:

The note is translated below:

Thank you for helping free me from a problem that had accompanied me for years. The effort was worth it. The proof is before you [meaning the picture].

Thank you again.

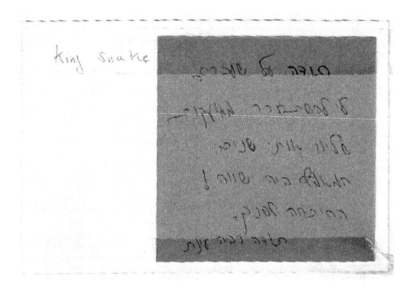

Treating OCD

Let us now turn our attention to obsessive compulsive disorder (OCD).

Obsessive compulsive disorder falls under the larger category of anxiety disorders, because the underlying disturbance is felt by the patient as anxiety. Obsessions are uncontrolled anxiety provoking *thoughts*. Compulsions are anxiety provoking *behaviours*. These behaviours usually have to be repeated many times before the person can move on.

Compulsions and obsessions fall into several categories:

Checking

- People will check potentially dangerous situations, like checking if the gas is turned off or checking if the door is locked; these checking compulsions are strongest at night before people go to bed, because when they are asleep, they have no control, and the danger, they imagine, is greater. The act of checking is repeated over and over four, five, six times, or more.

Contamination

- Because of fear of lethal germs, people will wash their hands over and over. Excessive washing leads to conspicuously red or chapped hands. They assiduously avoid touching unclean objects.

Ruminations/Intrusive Thoughts

- These are terms for unwanted thoughts or obsessions.

Hoarding

- This is collecting papers that have no special value and saving them for an unlimited period of time. People think it may have value in the future, so they fear getting rid of it. Hoarders have been known to collect so many items that their home is filled to capacity with clutter and they have no place to eat or sleep, resulting in their moving out.
- Psychologists now think that hoarding maybe different from other OCD symptoms, but in the final analysis, it makes no difference. The treatments of choice for this problem are the same as for other OCD problems: medication and CBT treatment.

Symmetry and Ordering

If they see things are out of order, they feel uncomfortable and anxious. I once interviewed a person with OCD, and he seemed distracted when I spoke with him. Finally, he asked if he could straighten a closed umbrella that was on the couch. When he did, he was relieved and better focused.

Such people cannot pass an object that seems out of place without rearranging it and putting it in its place.

They must arrange their shoes and clothes in way that seems correct to them. This compulsive need can greatly interfere with getting household jobs completed; everything must be done perfectly.

Religious Sufferers

Scrupulosity, for Catholics and Protestants, is characterised by pathological guilt about moral or religious issues. It is personally distressing and objectively dysfunctional, and it is often accompanied by significant impairment in social functioning.

The symptoms of some religiously observant Jews who have OCD take on a religious flavour. Since the believing Jew has many commandments to fulfil daily (dietary laws, laws of family purity, and so on), the compulsions impact on the fulfilment of these commandments. Contamination fears are translated into fear of not washing according to the law or of not immersing in the ritual bath as required. It also manifests itself in excessive concern for mixing milk and meat in the kitchen, requiring them to frequently wash their hands.

Ordering symptoms are directed to having one's phylacteries in the right place or placing Hebrew holy books right side up if they are not so.

Checking fears for religious women can manifest in worries that when they check themselves during the days leading to their ritual bath obligation, if may not have been done right

Obsessions can revolve around such doubts as "Do I really believe in G-d or really believe in what the Torah says?" People who live a very observant life, when all their behaviour is governed by Jewish law, can have these fears, and they are very anxiety-provoking.

Treating OCD

When we first meet patients, we ask why they have come and what they want help with. We take nothing for granted; we want to hear in their words what they see as the problem.

As we said about phobias, we ask patients in what way their lives will be different – better – after successful therapy. Specifically, what will they be able to do that they can't do now. This becomes our behavioural goal in treatment.

We give them a questionnaire to fill out. It is the OC Inventory Revised:

The following statements refer to experiences that many people have in their everyday lives. Circle the number that best describes how much that experience has distressed or bothered you during the past month. The numbers refer to the following verbal labels:

0	1	2	3	4
Not at all	A little	Moderately	A lot	Extremely

1. I have saved up so many things that they get in the way. 0 1 2 3 4
2. I check things more often than necessary 0 1 2 3 4

3. I get upset if objects are not arranged properly. 0 1 2 3 4

4. I feel compelled to count while I am doing things. 0 1 2 3 4

5. I find it difficult to touch an object when I know it has been touched by strangers or certain people. 0 1 2 3 4

6. I find it difficult to control my thoughts 0 1 2 3 4

7. I collect things that I don't need. 0 1 2 3 4

8. I repeatedly check doors, windows, drawers, etc. 0 1 2 3 4

9. I get upset if others change the way I have arranged things. 0 1 2 3 4

10. I feel I have to repeat certain numbers. 0 1 2 3 4

11. I sometimes have to wash my hands or clean myself simply because I feel contaminated. 0 1 2 3 4

12. I am upset by unpleasant thoughts against my will. 0 1 2 3 4

13. I avoid throwing things away because I am afraid I might need them later. 0 1 2 3 4

14. I repeatedly check gas/water taps and light switches after turning them off. 0 1 2 3 4

15. I need things to be arranged in a certain order 0 1 2 3 4

16. I feel there are good and bad numbers. 0 1 2 3 4

17. I wash my hands more often and longer than necessary 0 1 2 3 4

18. I frequently get nasty thoughts and have difficulty getting rid of them. 0 1 2 3 4

Grading

Add the numbers; if the total is 4 or below, it is normal. If it is 5–7, that is borderline; 8 or above is a problem; he should seek help.

This questionnaire should be given at the beginning of therapy and at the end to see if any problems remain. It can also be given in the course of therapy to see if progress is being made.

Applying EX/RP to OCD

As we said above, anxiety disorders are best dealt with by the exposure/ response prevention technique. We can apply it to compulsive behaviours as well.

This means that we encourage patients to expose themselves to the anxiety-provoking situation (e.g., touching dirt) and then prevent the response (which is to wash their hands). As we said regarding treating phobias, no situation which is frightening to patients should be forced on them against their will. They must know what they are expected to do and what we plan to do, and they must agree to do it.

Here too, we work with a fear hierarchy. Patients tell us or write out a series of situations (regarding dirt) which they then order from the least disturbing to the most disturbing. We begin with the least disturbing

I have found that most people who come for help for OCD have issues with washing and cleanliness, no matter what other OCD symptoms they may have. It is for that reason that I think it is important to focus on reducing the patient's need for hand washing.

After hearing them out, we begin with having them record at home each time they wash their hands. They record the date in the first column; the time they washed in the second column; and in the third column the reason they washed (e.g., after the bathroom or after coming in from outside).

The recording serves two purposes. First, it gives a better sense of their washing problem, both the number of times and also the reasons they wash. Some may be normal reasons, while many will not be. The second purpose is to help them become more aware of their excessive washing. That alone may help reduce the number of times they wash.

At the next session, we go over the list to find those times that were really unnecessary, like "coming in from the outside" or "before going into the kitchen." We discuss this and hear their reasons for washing and their fears if they didn't wash. We show them how others wash and try to convince them to reduce some of these times. Since water is their saviour and their compulsion, we can tell them to use a paper towel to wipe their hands instead of washing, if they feel it is necessary. This move from water to paper towel will make it easier to give up the paper towel as well.

The rule is, unless you actually see something on your hand, then no washing, even if you *think* you feel the dirt. Only seeing what others can see is justification for cleaning one's hands.

We then begin our homework challenges. We ask that they continue recording but this time not to wash, for example, when they come in from the outside. We wait for their consent try to encourage them and build them up to the challenge.

The next session, we will ask how they did with their challenge. They probably did 50-50. They should be asked first what helped them succeed when they did and what caused them to fail when that happened.

Our sessions continue this way, focusing on their challenge but also leaving time to bring up other matters that concern them. It is good to ask them about their overall feeling during the past week – more tense, less anxiety, or whatever, and ask what the cause might be for any change.

Identifying the Core Fear

To achieve a faster, more generalised therapeutic effect and improve prognosis for relapse prevention, it is essential to identify early on in therapy the underlying core fear that may be contributing to the abundance of ritual presentations. Here are some common examples of obsessive core fears that can feed the sufferer's fears:

- being responsible for harming others
- going "crazy"
- being a bad or immoral person
- contracting a fatal disease and dying
- for religious people, going to hell

It is crucial to identify the precise core fear, which may not be apparent at first. For example, one patient with obsessions related to the possibility of being gay was not very distressed by an imagined scenario of having a torrid gay love affair; rather, his core fear was that he would realise he was gay, come out to his family, and as a result lose the people in his life he loved the most.

Dealing with a Core Fear

The best way to deal with a core fear is by imaginary exposure: guided imagery. We construct a scene where all the worse things happen just as he feared. An example could be for one who checks the door to see if it's locked, he decides not to double-check and face his anxiety. But just that night, a burglar enters his home and harms his wife and child before escaping. His wife blames him for being "irresponsible."

Imagining this scene over and over until his anxiety levels go down will help him overcome this core fear: not being responsible and disaster happens as a consequence.

By treating the core fear, we make it easier to treat the specific compulsions and reduce the chance that other related compulsions will pop up after others are treated.

Seeking Reassurance

A common characteristic of sufferers from OCD is their need for reassurance, from those near to them, family, or therapists, that everything will be okay. But as we say below such reassurance seeking is itself a compulsion and giving reassurance does not help the person in the long run, in fact it makes his situation more imbedded.

Involved persons provide reassurance because they (1) believe it is helpful to the patient and shows they care about their loved one, (2) lack understanding that it interferes with treatment, (3) are negatively reinforced for providing reassurance because it decreases conflict with the patient, or (4) lack knowledge of alternative responses.

The assurance-seeking itself is a compulsion. Rarely will a one-time reassurance help the patient for more than a very short time. Reassurance is not only not helpful; it is also harmful. It is harmful because it reinforces the need for more reassurance in the future. So while it gives patients a brief immediate relief, it insures that they will need more and more reassurances in the future; in other words, it strengthens their doubts.

Reassurance should be avoided at all costs. The best way to do this is to tell sufferers, during a quiet time, when they are not asking for reassurance, that if they ask in the future, you will tell them no.

You may add, "I do this because it may seem helpful to you if I reassure you, but it is really harmful. So I do not answer because I want to help you."

Dealing with the Family of the Patient

There are two main ways family members may be involved negatively with the sufferer:

1) Offering reassurance. As is mentioned above, reassurance has negative consequences. It is recommended to work with patients and their close others to develop a plan for how they should respond to the patient's reassurance seeking. Not only will this plan help relieve involved individuals of the burden of managing the patient's OCD, it will strengthen the patient's ability to prevent rituals across different contexts, which optimises the likelihood of treatment success.

2) Serving the person's compulsion by proxy. Many individuals with OCD recruit family members to participate in avoidance and compulsions. These behaviours have been termed "family accommodation." It is important to teach family members that they should refrain from performing "OCD by proxy"; for example, by washing the patient's clothes so she does not have to confront the OCD-related distress associated with dirty laundry. The family person should just refuse to do these things. The refusal should be done without anger, just matter-of-factly.

Exposure and Response Repetition

Before we go further, I would add another, as yet unreported, technique for dealing with compulsions. I call it Exposure and Response Repetition (EX/ RR). It works this way, taking hand washing compulsion as an example: we tell patients that they should try not to wash their hands but if they cannot overcome the urge to wash their hands, they should wash them as much as necessary until they feel relief. And then they should wash them three more times. This counterintuitive instruction will certainly surprise them, but they are urged to do it. I tell patients, "I cannot ask you to do what you cannot do, but I can ask you to do what you may not want to do."

This instruction turns the compulsion on its head. Before, it was an act they could not control; now, it is an act which they do control. Once they gain some control over it, they can use that control to stop the hand washing. In addition, of course, it can be felt as a punishment. They do not want to wash again. So as a punishment to previous washings, it can help reduce the urge to wash. There is empirical evidence for the effectiveness of this approach (Rabavilis et al., *J Behavior Therapy and Experimental Psychiatry.* 1977).

Rabavilis reported using this technique with four checking compulsive patients. The four patients were instructed that when they felt compelled to check more than once, they were to continue checking beyond the point imposed on them by their compulsion. They were to continue checking another fifty times. His unexpected finding was that not one of the patients performed this technique because not one of them was interested in checking beyond the one time.

So we see that doing the compulsion more than they themselves want to do it was an inhibiter of the compulsion itself. Strategic therapists call this "prescribing the symptom."

I have used this technique with several OCD patients. The results are described in my article, "What's broken with CBT treatment of OCD and how to fix it" (*American J of Psychotherapy* 63, 1).

The question can be asked, why does this work? How can we understand it psychologically?

One explanation is, as we said above, the repetition beyond the compulsion is a voluntary act. It is a voluntary act and one they do not want to do; it can act as a punishment. As a punishment, it reduces the chance that the compulsion will be done in the future.

Another explanation is based on the concept of satiation.

The graph below is a record of an institutionalised psychotic woman, who hoarded towels in her room. She was given two towels a week but continued to ask for and take additional towels on the average of twenty a week. The intervention started on the seventh week after baseline observation. Then the staff brought to her room more and more towels, even if she didn't ask for them. In the beginning, she thanked them, but after the towels filled her room, to the total of 640 towels, she begged them not to bring any more. Then she herself began removing towels from her room until she had only two or three towels.

This is an example of satiation; when the positive reinforcement reached satiation, then it became an aversive consequence.

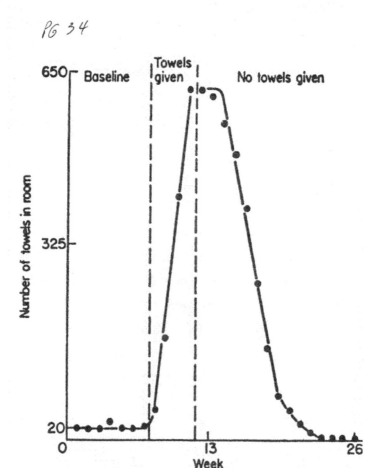

This too may explain why RE/RR reduces the compulsion. The compulsive act reached satiation and then became aversive.

Dealing with Obsessions

As a rule, obsessions are more difficult than compulsions to treat, because they are not behaviours, which can more easily be prevented. The therapist has no direct contact with the patient's obsession. Patients must report their obsession for the therapist to be aware of it.

This is true for pure obsessions (referred to as Pure O) where no behavioural compulsions can be found. But as a rule, compulsions usually follow obsessions; when searched out diligently, by questioning the patient, compulsions can be located.

Let us assume that we are dealing with a case of Pure O; what can we do?

Obsessions have a similar format as compulsions. With compulsions, patients feel an uncontrollable urge to do a compulsive behaviour. Then they more wilfully decide to repeat it in order to relieve their anxiety. In other words, while a compulsion begins involuntarily, it continues voluntarily. Therapy then focuses on the more voluntary compulsion (the repeated act) in response prevention.

In obsessions, the problem begins with an involuntary thought (obsession), and then the person consciously and wilfully tries to combat it with another thought. For example, she may think she will kill her child; she then thinks, *No, I won't; it's not true.* The second thought is to undo the first thought. It is done voluntarily. In treatment, we first make patients aware of this two-step process and then ask them not to undo their obsession.

This may be done directly by fighting the urge to undo, or it can be done more directly by accepting the obsession, by thinking, *Yes, I might kill my child.*

Concluding Therapy

Both therapist and patient decide if the therapeutic goals have been achieved. If they have – meaning the patient can do all or most of the behavioural goals set out at the beginning – then concluding the therapy is appropriate. It would be wise to have the patient fill out the OC questionnaire again and compare it to the first questionnaire.

Patients should be told to expect some setbacks: "Setbacks are very common. They do not mean that you haven't succeeded in treatment. It means you have. Otherwise, if you didn't progress, you couldn't regress!" Setbacks are temporary bumps in the road. When they occur, patients should use the CBT skills they used in therapy.

Treating Panic Attacks

A panic attack (PA) is a discrete period in which there is the sudden onset of intense apprehension, fearfulness, or terror, often associated with feelings of impending doom. During these attacks, symptoms such as shortness of breath, palpitations, chest pain or discomfort, choking or smothering sensations, and fear of "going crazy" or losing control are present.

A panic disorder means the individual suffers these attacks over a period of time and not as a one-time episode.

The definition above is quite dry and academic; more to the point is that a panic attack is an unimaginably terrifying experience, as if one were a moment before dying. It has the power to induce "one-time" learning. That means that if people have an attack in a certain place (supermarket, lunchroom etc.) just one attack will teach them to fear that place, and they will refuse to go back there.

According to statistical studies, about 3 per cent of the population suffers from such attacks. This disorder was difficult to treat effectively until medications and CBT came along. The advantage of CBT over medication is that there are no unwanted side effects; equally as important, patients can learn the CBT treatment and apply it themselves if need be in the future.

CBT for Panic Attacks

The most studied and empirically proven treatment for PA is called Panic Control Treatment (PCT), constructed by David Barlow and colleagues.

Panic Control Treatment

This is a three-component model in which the dimensions of anxiety are grouped into physical, cognitive, and behavioural categories. The physical component includes bodily changes (e.g., neurological, hormonal, cardiovascular) and their associated somatic sensations (e.g., shortness of breath, palpitations, light-headedness). The cognitive component consists of the rational and irrational thoughts, images, and impulses that accompany anxiety or fear (e.g., thoughts of dying, images of losing control, impulses to run). The behavioural component contains the things people do when they are anxious or afraid (e.g., pacing, leaving or avoiding a situation, carrying a safety object).

A variety of techniques are used to treat the complexity of a panic attack:

1) Patients are taught the body's normal reaction to fear, like increased heart rate, perspiration, light-headedness. Explaining the body's normal reaction to fear acts to demystify panic attacks.
   When the body reacts this way, individuals look around to see what the danger is. But when they cannot find a real danger outside of themselves, they begin to look inside. They conclude (wrongly) that something in their body is telling them they are in danger – maybe a fatal heart attack. This heightens their already fearful state. Therapists use this real-life example to show how our thoughts influence our emotions.

2) Having laid this foundation, PCT then teaches patients skills for controlling each of the three components of anxiety. To manage

some of the physical aspects of anxiety, such as sensations due to hyperventilation (e.g., light-headedness and tingling sensations) or muscle tension (e.g., trembling and dyspnoea), patients are taught slow, diaphragmatic breathing or progressive muscle relaxation. To reduce anxiety-exacerbating thoughts and images, patients are taught to critically examine, on the basis of past experience and logical reasoning, their estimations of the likelihood that a feared event will occur, the probable consequences if it should occur, and their ability to cope with it. In addition, they are helped to design and conduct behavioural experiments to test their predictions.

3) To change maladaptive anxiety and fear behaviours, patients are taught to engage in graded therapeutic exposure to cues they associate with panic attacks. The exposure component of standard PCT (called "interoceptive exposure") focuses primarily on internal cues – specifically, frightening bodily sensations. During exposure, patients deliberately provoke physical sensations like smothering, dizziness, or tachycardia by means of exercises such as breathing through a straw, spinning, or vigorous exercise. These exercises are done initially during treatment sessions, with therapist modelling, and subsequently by patients at home. As patients become less afraid of the sensations, more naturalistic activities are assigned, such as drinking caffeinated beverages, having sexual intercourse, or watching scary movies.

Exposure to external cues (traditional situational exposure) is not systematically addressed in standard PCT, although as patients begin to apply the techniques they have learned, they are encouraged to gradually re-enter situations they have been avoiding. PCT focuses on panic and not on agoraphobia (which we will discuss below). Therefore, the developers did not include a more systematic situational exposure component in

PCT because they wanted to focus initially on the experience of panic attacks, rather than on avoidance behaviour, since this had not been done previously. An optional agoraphobia supplement was developed later for use with patients who have significant situational avoidance.

Further and more detailed information about PCT can be found in protocols by Barlow and Craske.

Agoraphobia

Agoraphobia literally means "fear of the marketplace." But in fact, it means fear of leaving one's home alone. As can be imagined, such a fear is terribly disabling. A housewife must wait until her husband comes home in order to do her shopping. Social events are also avoided, even with a companion, because crowds have to be avoided. The reason for this is that the basis of agoraphobia is fear of having a panic attack, and in such a case, the person wants to be able to flee as quickly as possible. A crowd impedes such an escape.

CBT treatment for agoraphobia is based on exposure and response prevention. It is a very effective treatment. People who have been homebound for twenty-five years because of agoraphobia can overcome the problem with CBT. For effective treatment, therapists must be willing to leave their offices and go out with their patients to meet their challenges in real life.

Social Phobia

Social phobia has been defined as the "fear of behaving publicly due to fear of being judged unfavourably." The most common social phobia is fear of public speaking, but the phobia can manifest itself in the fear of writing in front of others and the fear of eating with others present.

The fear is basically the fear of fear: the fear that others will notice that the person is nervous. Therefore, the fear of eating is because holding one's shaking fork or spoon can show that person's nervousness, likewise in writing before others. I once treated a sixty-year-old woman whose social phobia manifested itself by a fear of writing. She was sitting with a group of friends, and they decided to send a get-well card to one of their group who was in the hospital; when her turn to sign her name came, this woman was so overcome by anxiety that she ended up in the hospital herself.

Treating social phobia is usually more difficult than other phobias because the feared "object" is other people, and we cannot be sure their response will be benign. Fear of elevators, for example, is easier to treat by exposure because the elevator's response is always the same.

The usual CBT approach has been exposure to a graded scale of less to more fearful situations, like talking to two people at a time; then three; then four or more.

Another technique, which takes much courage but can be very effective, is to have the person explain her fear to the audience she is speaking to before she starts her actual speech. She would say, "I have to admit to you that I have a fear of speaking to such crowds and the fear causes my voice to weaken, and my hands to shake, and me to perspire. So please excuse me if this happens as I talk to you."

Since the underlying fear is the fear of being discovered, such an admission makes "discovery" no longer possible, since the patient has already told the truth. This creates a win-win situation; if she is, in fact, nervous, she can say, "I told you so." If she is not nervous, that certainly is a win.

Post-Traumatic Stress Disorder

DSM V defines PTSD this way:

"Diagnostic criteria for PTSD include a history of exposure to a traumatic event that meets specific stipulations and symptoms from each of four symptom clusters: intrusion, avoidance, negative alterations in cognitions and mood, and alterations in arousal and reactivity. The fifth criterion concerns duration of symptoms; the seventh assesses functioning; and, the eighth criterion clarifies symptoms as not attributable to a substance or co-occurring medical condition. The condition must last at least a month to be considered PTSD."

This is the only anxiety disorder that is precipitated by a real-life, life-threatening event. Other anxiety disorders are precipitated either by internal physiological trauma (panic attack) or imagined trauma.

Normal functioning individuals can be turned into emotional cripples following a real-life trauma. The disorder can last decades if not treated successfully.

The good news is that several psychological treatments have emerged in the past decades that have proven to be effective.

Because treatment is complex and the problem is quite serious, I will not discuss actual treatment processes here. I will suggest some of the elements in the successful treatment packages. There is no royal road to becoming a successful PTSD therapist. Therapists who want to learn a particular therapeutic approach must study with an experienced PTSD therapist.

Here are some important elements in therapy:

1) **Prolonged exposure.** All exposure to anxiety increases the anxiety in the first stage. Eventually, with continued exposure, the anxiety subsides. It can take anywhere from a half-hour to ninety minutes. If exposure is stopped before the anxiety subsides, the problem is increased, because patients again experienced anxiety without relief. But if exposure lasts long enough – even an hour or more – then the anxiety will subside and patients will experience relief from their trauma.

2) **Cognitive restructuring.** Therapy must help patients experience the anxiety with a new, less-threatening understanding. For example, a rape victim may have blamed herself all the years after her trauma because she may, in some way, have had sexual pleasure during the rape. She must restructure this misunderstanding to realise she was forced into the rape and not free to escape it. Relieving her misperceived guilt is an important element in cure.

Recommended Reading

David Barlow's *Handbook of Psychological Disorders*, the chapter on PTSD. Edna B. Foa, et al. "Randomised Trial of Prolonged Exposure for Posttraumatic Stress Disorder with and without Cognitive Restructuring: Outcome at Academic and Community Clinics." *Journal of Consulting and Clinical Psychology* 73, 5, 953–964, 2005.

Depression

We now leave the anxiety spectrum of disorders and turn to a common psychological problem: depression.

Cognitive Approach to Depression

Aaron Beck developed the cognitive approach with his seminal work with depressed patients. His approach can be exemplified by the transcript from this cognitive therapy session (by Judy Beck in her book, *Cognitive Therapy Basics and Beyond* with permission):

This is the fourth session of an eighteen-year-old female college student who was depressed.

Therapist: Okay, Sally, you said you wanted to talk about a problem with finding a part-time job?

Patient: I need the money ... but I don't know.

T. (Noticing the patient's sad look) What's going through your mind right now?

P. I won't be able to handle the job.

T. And how does that make you feel?

P. Sad. Really low.

T. So you have thought, *I won't be able to handle the job*. And that thought makes you feel sad. What's the evidence that you won't be able to work?

P. Well, I'm having trouble just getting through my classes.

T. Okay. What else?

P. I don't know ... I'm so tired. It's hard to make myself even go and look for a job, much less go to work every day.

T. In a minute, we'll look at that. Maybe it's actually harder for you at this point to go out and *investigate* jobs than it would be for you to go to a job that you already had. In any case, any other evidence that you couldn't handle a job, assuming you could get one?

P. No, I can't think of any.

T. Any evidence on the other side? That you *might* be able to handle a job?

Summary: We can see at least two things the therapist did here:

1) The therapist showed the patient the connection between her thoughts and her feelings.

2) The therapist directed the patient to take action and to get a job.

This in fact is close to what Aaron Beck has written about his cognitive therapy:

> "Intervention with behavioral techniques can enter and change self-destructive behavior. The most commonly used behavioral techniques include scheduling activities that include mastery and pleasure exercises, self-reliance training, etc. The scheduling of activities is frequently used in the early stages of cognitive therapy to counteract loss of motivation, hopelessness and excessive rumination." (Barlow, p. 281).

Beck's idea here has been the basis for a new CBT treatment for depression termed behavioural activism, which has proven to be even more effective than Beck's cognitive therapy.

Behavioural Activism for Depression

The classic text for behavioural activism is *Behavioral Activism: A Clinician's Guide*, by C. R. Martell, S. Dimidjian, and Ruth Herman-Dunn.

In it, they outline in great detail their therapy for depression. The underlying theory is that depressed people have less motivation and thus shy away from social interactions or other activities that they enjoyed in the past. This lack of action feeds on itself and deepens the depression.

Thus, their therapy is basically to find those activities, solitary or interpersonal, that the person enjoyed in the past.

A proactive daily schedule is planned having the patient engage gradually in more and more pleasant activities. Such physical, mental, and social activity will pull patients out of their depression. The authors are very orderly and follow a ten-point program they call "the core principles":

Principle 1. The key to changing how people feel is helping change what they do.

Principle 2. Changes in life can lead to depression; short-term coping strategies may keep people stuck over time.

Principle 3. The clues to figuring out what will be antidepressant for a particular client lie in what precedes and what follows the client's important behaviour.

Principle 4. Structure and schedule activities that follow a plan, not a mood.

Principle 5. Change will be easier when starting small.

Principle 6. Emphasise activities which are naturally reinforcing.

Principle 7. Act as a coach.

Principle 8. Emphasise a problem-solving empirical approach, and recognise that all results are useful.

Principle 9. Don't just talk, do.

Principle 10. Troubleshoot possible and actual barriers to activities.

It should be pointed out that such a program cannot be carried out effectively in a clinic. Therapists (or an assistant) must accompany patients in real-life situations. They must encourage, even prod, patients to get up and act. Left to themselves, they probably wouldn't do much of the homework assignments. The authors suggest that the full program could take a half-year, with once-a-week sessions.

Assertive Training

No book on CBT would be complete without a section on assertive training. Assertive training is product of the CBT approach. Andrew Salter first introduced the idea in the 1950s. Later, Wolpe included it in his work with people with phobias. For reasons that are not all clear, when patients learn to be assertive, it has been found to elevate various phobias.

Assertive training is also a central part of increasing self-esteem.

It improves interpersonal relations, including spousal relations.

What Is Assertive Behaviour?

Assertive behaviour is behaviour enables a person to act in his own best interests, to stand up for himself without undue anxiety, to express his honest feeling comfortably, or to exercise his own rights without denying the rights of others.

Let it be clear at the outset that assertive behaviour is not aggressive behaviour. As the definition says, it is assertive behaviour *without* denying the rights of others. Such behaviour enables individuals to better achieve their goals in interpersonal interactions, while aggressive behaviour usually fails to do so, besides causing other interpersonal problems.

Diagnosing Nonassertive Behaviour

To see if patients are nonassertive, we can ask them to answer how they would react in several hypothetical situations:

1) Suppose you want to sell a book for $5. A mere acquaintance says she needs the book and can't find it anywhere but only has $3 to pay for it. You know you can easily get $5. What would you do?

2) Suppose a mere acquaintance asks you to go with him to eat. He might not go otherwise, but you've just eaten. What would you do?

3) You are studying for an exam; a good friend asks you to go to a concert with her. What would you do?

4) You are standing in line for a while for a movie ticket; as you get close to the window, some friends come and ask if they could go ahead of you. What would you do?

5) You lend a friend $100 for two weeks. The two weeks come and go, and he hasn't paid or said anything. When you ask for the payment, he asks, "Do you really need it now?" What would you say?

It is clear what the nonassertive answers are. On this basis, one can begin a conversation with the patient regarding assertiveness training.

Let's begin by quoting an interchange between a patient (P) and therapist (T) (from *Behavior Therapy,* Masters, J.C., et al.):

> T. From what you've been saying, it seems like you feel a lot of resentment and anger towards your brother-in-law. What do you think about feeling like that? I mean, is it a good or pleasant way to feel?
> P. Well, no. Sometimes I feel I'm going to lose control and hit him. That would be terrible.
> T. What else do you feel about him?
> P. Like I said, I'm pretty upset and nervous, and when I go over my sister's house for dinner, I don't feel like eating. I don't want to offend my sister so I eat, but afterwards, I feel like throwing up.

T. So, in other words, your brother-in-law's way of acting makes you angry and anxious and even sick to your stomach? Sounds like you are pretty miserable around him.

P. Yes, pretty miserable. Like I was saying, he's not the only one, but it's worse around him.

T. Just pretend for a minute that you were the sort of person who could tell him off, whenever he was bothering you. Whenever he was on your back, bullying you the way he does. How would you feel then?

P. Well, if I did tell him off, he'd say something to hurt my feelings. It wouldn't be worth it.

T. But suppose you were so effective at telling him how you felt that he really got the message and left you alone and even treated you with admiration and respect. How do you suppose you would feel then?

P. That's hard to imagine. If I could do it – I mean beat him at his own game – I'd feel a lot better. I just want him to leave me alone, and I would enjoy visiting my sister a lot more. But I don't think I could ever do it … I'm just not that way.

T. When you say you're "not that way," do you mean you just aren't comfortable being aggressive and maybe hurting other people's feelings?

P. Yeah, I mean I don't like when other people treat *me* that way. Do you know what I mean?

T. I think I do, and I really see your point. You don't like it when your brother-in-law bullies you, and you don't want to be a bully. Fair enough. But you know, being assertive is not the same as being aggressive. Aggressive is like you don't give a damn about how other people feel. When you're being assertive, you do care about how others feel, but you also care about how yourself feel.

P. I guess I can see the difference. Being assertive isn't about pulling people down. Hmmm. I don't know, maybe telling him how I feel would be the right thing to do.

T. Look, I don't want to play G-d and tell what is right and what is wrong. But I *will* say that you'll be a lot more honest if you tell him how you feel. And if you're like most people, you'll feel better afterwards. Especially if you say it in a way that doesn't make him feel like some kind of monster. And you know something else? There is a good possibility that your brother-in-law doesn't even realise how he's getting to you. If you make him aware of it, then he has a choice.

P. You almost make it sound like I'm doing him a favour.

T. I wasn't thinking along those lines but that is a very good point. He may be bullying other people ... you know, turning them off and not even knowing it.

P. I think he does. I really think he does. Maybe I could help him [Laughs].

T. That is quite possible. But don't lose track of yourself in the process. The main thing about being assertive is that you feel better and probably like yourself more. And your brother-in-law will take you more seriously. Being nonassertive can be very self-defeating.

P. Yeah, self-defeating. That's a good way to put it. But the thing is, I always get tense and clam up when anyone criticises me and especially when they make fun of me. You mean I'd be better off if I made up my mind to ... speak up?

T. Yes, there are some things we can do to help you express your feelings.

The therapist then explains the outlines of assertive training. He tells him that role playing in the safe confines of the clinic is a good way to learn assertiveness. The therapist explains that assertiveness lowers one's overall anxiety and can therefore be helpful in reducing anxiety in other situations he fears, like claustrophobia or other phobias.

Role Playing: Behavioural Rehearsal

It cannot be stressed too much how important role playing is in teaching assertive skills. Since it is done in the nonthreatening confines of the therapist's office, patients can be observed as they try out new modes of behaviour. It is an excellent teaching opportunity. The clients first "play" themselves as they react to a therapist-suggested situation. The therapist sees the problems they have acting assertively. It is interesting to note that even in the office, far away from a real-life situation, their nonassertive habits nevertheless come to the fore. Then the therapist role-plays how patients should respond assertively. This goes back and forth until they feel comfortable behaving assertively. Then anticipated situations in the patients' lives are brought up, and they are taught how to assertively respond to them (like to the brother-in-law in the last dialogue).

There are certain behavioural components to assertive communication. They include eye contact; facial expression; general posture; and leaning the body towards or away from the person we talking to. There are also aspects of talking that are important in assertiveness, like how soon one responds; how loud one talks; how much one says; how smooth the speech is. All of these can be learned; they must be learned. They contribute to the overall power of the message.

We now turn to some specific assertive responses that can be learned.

In his book, *Conditioned Reflex Therapy,* Salter pointed out the following behavioural exercises:

- The use of *feeling talk:* "I really love the warm weather" or "I can't stand spinach."
- The use of *facial talk.* Using appropriate facial expressions that go with what one is saying: smiling when you speak about happy events and so on.
- Practice in expressing contradictory opinions when one disagrees.
- Practice using "I" in your sentences; for example, "I feel warm in here" as opposed to "Isn't it warm in here?"
- Practice in agreeing when one is complimented. For example, on getting a compliment on your nice-looking clothes, say, "Yes, I like it too," not, "What? This old thing!"
- Practice in acting spontaneously without much forethought.

The Broken Record Technique

The purpose of assertive training is to help people relate as equals to those around them. But in fact, certain assertive techniques enable them to come from an inferior position to a superior one. The broken record technique is an example of this.

I will relate an experience that happened to me and how I used the broken record to get what I needed, though I was in an inferior position.

My car needed repairs, so I took it to my garage. The boss said it would be ready by noon. I was teaching in the university on one side of the city in the afternoon but could pick up my car on the way to my clinic on the opposite side of town. When I called the garage, they said it wasn't ready yet but would be later in the day. So I took a cab to my office. At 4.45, my wife phoned me to say the garage called and I had to pick up the car before they closed at five. I couldn't do that because I had clients scheduled and I couldn't cancel at the last minute. I called the garage, and he explained that my car was ready but I must pick it up before five o'clock, when he closed.

He said he'd wait until 5.15 but no later. Otherwise, I wouldn't get my car until Sunday. It was Thursday, but the garage was closed on Friday and Saturday. So I said (using the broken record formula), "I understand, but I can't come now, and I need the car tomorrow." He repeated his conditions, and then I said, "I understand, but I can't come now, and I need the car tomorrow." He repeated once more and then yelled into the phone, "I'm not your servant!" I ignored that remark and said, "I understand, but I can't come now, and I need the car tomorrow." Finally, he slammed the phone down and disconnected. I sat there, puzzled and frustrated. It didn't work, I thought. Then on Friday, my wife got a call at home from the garage. He said, "I happen to be in the garage today; you can come and get your car. I will be leaving at 1 p.m."

My wife said she couldn't come then, she was in the middle of cooking, but she would come later. She did and got the car.

Now let's analyse what happened here.

The first question is, why did the garage man call me on Friday? I didn't know and wouldn't know if he was there or not.

Another question regards how the broken record helped.

The answer explores how the broken record did and did not do several important things:

1) I respected the garage man by simply saying, "I understand," at the beginning of each response. I was sort of seeing his side of things.

2) I never argued with him.

3) I didn't slip down to the personal level. When he said, "I am not your servant," I didn't even say, "No, I didn't mean that," which would have acknowledged his statement. I simply passed over it.

4) I did not suggest other solutions to the problem. I could have said, "Leave the car on the street. I have another set of keys; I'll pick it up later." Because that would have exposed me to his answer; he could have said he had no insurance for that. Then I would have to do what he said. So I said nothing.

That is why he called on Friday, even though he didn't have to, because I did not antagonise him; he was left with a guilty feeling.

In short, teaching a nonassertive patient the broken record technique can be very empowering.

A Variety of Psychological Problems and CBT Treatment

We will now look at a variety of problems that the therapist may deal with and see how the CBT approach deals with them.

Trichotillomania

Most humans pull, pluck, and pick at their hair, skin, and nails in small amounts. But when these behaviours become excessive, they are considered disorders and can cause a lot of suffering. Though not well known, these disorders affect millions of people of all ages. The good news is, treatment and support are available.

The problem of excessive and uncontrolled hair pulling is called trichotillomania.

Trichotillomania is similar to a compulsion, in that it is a repetitive behaviour which cannot be controlled by the person. But it is different from OCD in that there is usually no anxiety connected to this problem.

It is difficult to deal with this problem by the EX/RP technique because the act of pulling takes place so quickly and so easily; the object pulled – one's hair – is always available and close by. So we must find another technique suited to this problem.

Nathan Azrin and Richard Nunn authored the book *Habit Control in One Day*. Their treatment for tric is to first identify the times or situations when hair pulling happens most frequently. It may be before going to sleep or while reading a book or watching TV or in class during a lecture.

The common denominator of these various situations is that individuals are passive, and their hands are free. They first must keep a record of the times and situations when they pull their hair. A sample of two or three days is sufficient. This gives us a baseline for comparison once treatment begins. It also increases their awareness of their hair pulling.

Azrin and Nunn recommend that they hold something in their hands at these crucial times. Best is a hand grip that they can squeeze.

They continue to record the times they pull, plus the times they thought of pulling but did not.

The logic behind this technique is fairly obvious. One cannot do two different things with one hand. Of course, they could pull with their free hands. Recording will show if this happens. If it does, we must occupy both hands.

This technique will rapidly reduce the number of hair pulls per day. The problem may be to have the person do this consistently. If progress is slow, if it is a child, we can add a chart in which we give one point if he held the grip and two points if he didn't pull hair. The parent should set a goal in number of points that need to be reached in order to receive an inexpensive reward (e.g., pen) in a week or ten days, at the most. A more substantial reward can be given if the child has a good record (it need not be 100 per cent perfect; 80–90 per cent reduction) after six weeks.

The person (or parent) should obtain any meds or creams that enhance hair growth (massaging with castor oil and olive oil may help).

Photos of the different stages of hair growth should be taken and viewed by the patient to encourage motivation to continue working on the problem.

Let us look at another problem often discussed with a psychotherapist: insomnia.

Insomnia

Insomnia can be a very disturbing problem. People are frustrated when they can't fall asleep easily; they are tired and drowsy during the day and dread night-time and getting into bed.

There is a clear empirical, validated CBT treatment for this problem; it consists of several parts. We will review them.

First, as we always do, we request a sleep diary from patients. They record when they went to bed, when they think they fell asleep, and when they got out of bed in the morning. They also record if they napped during the day.

Sleep Restriction Therapy

The next step is called sleep restriction. No naps during the day are allowed. This is difficult because they will feel very tired; nevertheless, they should avoid naps at all costs. They should go to bed at midnight, not before, no matter how tired they feel. Patients report that this stage is the hardest. They are more tired than ever. Once patients report a good night's sleep – this may take 6 weeks of sleep restriction – they can start going to bed a half-hour earlier (11.30 p.m.). With good reports of sleep, the time is moved earlier and earlier to the person's satisfaction. They may want to go to sleep at 11 p.m. So that would be enough.

Then, a new stage is introduced, called stimulus control.

Stimulus Control Instructions

Stimulus control instructions are created by looking at patients' sleep habits and pinpointing different actions that may be inhibiting sleep. Patients are instructed not to spend time in their bedrooms when they aren't sleeping; they leave the bedroom when they aren't able to sleep, and they don't return until they are ready to sleep. This means that if they lie in bed for fifteen minutes and don't fall asleep, they must get out of bed and read or do housework until they feel tired, then they can return to bed.

The next stage is teaching sleep hygiene.

Sleep Hygiene Education

This means a customised list of things you should and should not do, in order to sleep. It often includes sleeping in a cool, dark room and avoiding caffeine, alcohol, and tobacco before bedtime. Sleep hygiene education is most helpful when tailored to an analysis of the patient's sleep/wake behaviours. The tailoring process allows clinicians to demonstrate the extent to which they comprehend the patient's individual circumstances (by knowing which items do and do not apply).

As an example, patients frequently watch their bedside clock to see how late it is. This should be avoided; it only adds to frustration. The clock should be removed. If it is necessary for the morning alarm, it can be placed under the bed.

Another bit of advice that may be helpful is not to exercise close to bedtime and not to do work before bed. It only revs you up. A relaxing activity should be a prelude to sleep; reading a novel or listening to music may be appropriate. The TV should not be in the bedroom; it associates being awake with bed.

The process also allows clinicians to critically review the rules.

The last stage of therapy is relapse prevention.

Relapse Prevention

This is an important element of cognitive behavioural therapy. Patients need to learn how to maintain what they've learned and prepare for the possibility of a future flare-up. They need to be reminded that lots of things may trigger a bout of insomnia; these are the main things one can do to protect against a new onset episode of chronic insomnia:

1. Don't compensate for sleep loss by sleeping during the day.
2. Start stimulus control procedures immediately.
3. Re-engage sleep restriction should the insomnia persist beyond a few days.

This is the final stage of therapy. Relapse prevention and learning the rules of the CBT treatment enables patients to manage further treatment – if necessary – by themselves.

Treating Serious Delinquent Behaviour

The problem of young delinquents can be grave and cause serious damage to people and objects.

The use of tokens (points for good behaviour) has been successfully used in such problems.

A case example (*Behavior Therapy*, Masters, J.C., et al.) is that of a thirteen-year-old boy who had been institutionalised since the age of nine for offences including stealing, starting fires, cruelty to animals and younger children, glue sniffing, breaking and entering, and smearing paint on the walls of the isolation room. He had compiled several different diagnoses such as psychopath and schizophrenia. During the year prior to the CBT program, he spent two hundred days in an isolation room. Upon examination, it was found that the isolation room was very ineffective because staff members felt sorry for the boy and brought him snacks (!), and other children could communicate with him through his window.

The contingency program lasted five months (a contingency program means that a person is rewarded with points contingent on positive behaviour and punished by fines – loss of points – for inappropriate behaviour). When the boy acted badly – according to clearly defined behaviours – he was sent to the isolation room for three hours.

For each hour of the day he was not in isolation (meaning he behaved), he received a token. If he stayed overnight outside the room, he received three tokens. The tokens were like money; he could exchange them for soda, cigarettes, trips to the city, and movies. As his behaviour improved, the challenges got harder. After two months, he had to stay out of the isolation room for two hours (not just one hour, as before) in order to earn a token. He also received a bonus of seven tokens if he was out of the room for a twenty-four-hour period. Finally, the time-out period was shortened to two hours instead of three so he could be outside longer and earn more points for positive behaviour.

In the end, isolation was rarer than before; eighteen times the first month, twelve times the last month. More importantly, the "crimes" committed were much less serious the last month than those in the first month: stealing from staff, fighting, sniffing glue, but in the last month, the offences were running in the dormitory, disrupting class, and insolence – all much more normative behaviours.

We see the power of consistent and pinpoint use of tokens in changing behaviour. In using tokens, we must be aware of several things:

1) Make the challenges easily achievable in the beginning.
2) Give the tokens immediately after the good behaviour.
3) Use fines less often than rewards; otherwise, the child is in debt early on and has no motivation to improve.
4) Relate to the child with respect and not anger, always.

Anger Management

Constructive Criticism

CBT is considered an effective treatment for those who can't control (or lose control of) their anger and abuse others, either verbally or physically.

The following are steps that many CBT therapists recommend:

1. Think before you speak.
In the heat of the moment, it's easy to say something you'll later regret. Take a few moments to collect your thoughts before saying anything – and allow others involved in the situation to do the same.

2. Once you're calm, express your anger.
As soon as you're thinking clearly, express your frustration in an assertive but nonconfrontational way. State your concerns and needs clearly and directly, without hurting others or trying to control them.

3. Get some exercise.
Physical activity can help reduce stress that can cause you to become angry. If you feel your anger escalating, go for a brisk walk or run, or spend time doing some other enjoyable physical activity.

4. Take a time-out.
Time-outs aren't just for kids. Give yourself short breaks during times of the day that tend to be stressful. A few moments of quiet time might help you feel better prepared to handle what's ahead, without getting irritated or angry.

5. Identify possible solutions.
Instead of focusing on what made you mad, work on resolving the issue at hand. Does your child's messy room drive you crazy? Close the door. Is your partner late for dinner every night? Schedule meals later in the evening – or agree to eat on your own a few times a week. Remind yourself that anger won't fix anything and might only make it worse.

6. Stick with "I" statements.
To avoid criticising or placing blame – which might only increase tension – use "I" statements to describe the problem. Be respectful and specific. For

example, say, "I'm upset that you left the table without offering to help with the dishes," instead of, "You never do any housework."

7. Don't hold a grudge.

Forgiveness is a powerful tool. If you allow anger and other negative feelings to crowd out positive feelings, you might find yourself swallowed up by your own bitterness or sense of injustice. But if you can forgive someone who angered you, you might both learn from the situation. It's unrealistic to expect everyone to behave exactly as you want at all times.

8. Use humour to release tension.

Lightening up can help diffuse tension. Use humour to help you face what's making you angry and any unrealistic expectations you have for how things should go. Avoid sarcasm, though; it can hurt feelings and make things worse.

9. Practise relaxation skills.

When your temper flares, put relaxation skills to work. Practise deep-breathing exercises, imagine a relaxing scene, or repeat a calming word or phrase, such as "Take it easy." You might also listen to music, write in a journal, or do a few yoga poses – whatever it takes to encourage relaxation.

10. Know when to seek help.

Learning to control anger is a challenge for everyone at times. Consider seeking help for anger issues if your anger seems out of control, causes you to do things you regret, or hurts those around you.

Constructive Criticism

As we look at this list of advice for controlling one's anger, we can see a serious weakness: what if the person doesn't do this? What happens then? These are suggestions, probably good ones as well, but just suggestions nevertheless. CBT treatment should deal with the "what-if" scenario: "What if the person forgets or ignores these suggestions?" The therapist has nothing to do but repeat them and encourage the person. Of course, the problem of anger is that it always seems to happen when we lose our cool, and by definition, at such times, we are less apt to remember these suggestions.

I would suggest a different approach to treating anger management.

It is comprised of two parts: one cognitive and one behavioural.

The cognitive part is how we see the event that got us angry. Instead of getting angry at the person who did something provocative, get angry at what he did, not who did it. This is similar to number 2 above. But the crucial element is the behavioural one. Remember CBT theory: anger is an operant (voluntary) behaviour. Such behaviours are influenced by what happens after they occur. To reduce a negative behaviour, we either punish or do extinction. Extinction is a slow process and not appropriate for abusive behaviour. An appropriate punishment would be a fine. If every time people get angry, they are fined, then their anger would stop. If they are serious about stopping their anger, I suggest they give the therapist $5,000 (as an example) up front to be kept in escrow for the patient, as a precondition for being in therapy. Each time they express anger, they lose $50. It is taken off the $5,000 they gave the therapist. At the end of therapy, they get back what is left of their $5,000.

This would be an authentic CBT program, based on learning theory.

Chapter 5

How to Diagnose a Problem and Make a Treatment Plan

This section may be the most important one in the book. In it, I outline the steps to diagnose a problem and then describe how to make a treatment plan.

As I said above, children's problems are easier to deal with than those of independent adults because they are usually in a closed social framework – either at home or in school (or an institution) – and can easily be monitored and controlled.

The following outline refers to dealing with children's problems (up to age seventeen years); it could, with a little thought, be adapted to an adult.

Steps to Diagnosis

1) **Behaviourally define** the problem you are dealing with.

2) **Observe** and **record** the instances when the behaviour occurs.

   Six days of observation are usually enough. This gives us a baseline with which we will compare the behaviour's occurrence after we begin treating it, with the baseline. In a week or two, we can see if we are on the right path.

3) With this information, we **prepare** for a treatment plan.

   Remember our equation A→B→C

   We look first at the observation record for A (antecedent conditions). Does the problem behaviour occur usually in a particular situation (e.g., a certain teacher, a certain time of day when he's tired, when he's sitting next to a particular student in class). If we find something consistent, then we consider changes in those conditions.

4) If we don't see any clue here, then we look at C (consequences). What happens *after* the behaviour occurs? Usually, bad behaviour draws attention and receives a reprimand or punishment. But in spite of reprimand or punishment, the bad behaviour continues. Why does it continue? Apparently, the reprimands are ineffective. But if the bad behaviour continues, this is evidence that something is reinforcing it; otherwise, it would die out. All behaviour dies out without reinforcement; the question is, where is there reinforcement? We are left with only one answer.

5) Since the behaviour didn't die, and continues, this means if he received reprimands and punishments, then these are reinforcing the behaviour. Even if that doesn't make sense, it is true. It is a consequence that comes after the behaviour and prolongs (instead of stopping) the behaviour.

6) So our treatment plan is clear; we (the teacher or parent) must stop the reprimands. This will be a plan of extinction. But we know extinction acts slowly, so we must combine it with reinforcement. That means the bad behaviour is ignored completely, and the teacher draws the student closer in conversation and compliments about anything except his bad behaviour.

7) Then we monitor our plan.

The graph below is of a sixteen-year-old student who cursed in class. The teacher recorded the number of times he cursed in a class period. Then as an intervention, she ignored the curses, not responding to them in any way. Instead, she found all kinds of ways to praise the student: for his homework or his success at soccer during recess, never referring to his cursing.

The graph shows clearly how ignoring bad behaviour had a dramatic and quick effect on his cursing: extinguishing it.

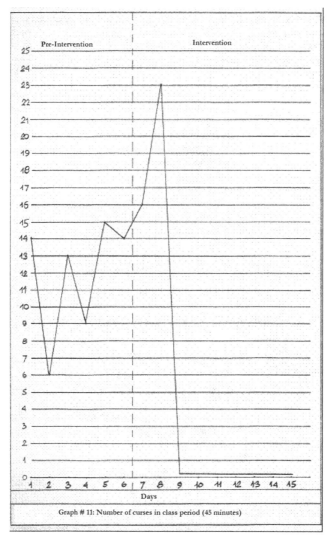

Graph # 11: Number of curses in class period (45 minutes)

But not all cases are so clear-cut. Some require some detective work to uncover the outside influence on the problem behaviour.

The following is from de Shazer (1988):

A family came to therapy to help their ten-year-old son overcome his bedwetting problem. The therapist asked if the boy ever woke up dry. Although they reported that occasionally he would wake up dry, they could not specify when this was. The boy's sister remembered that on Wednesdays, her brother was always dry. Further questioning revealed that on Wednesday mornings, the father woke the boy up; on other days, the mother woke him up. Then, in absence of the children, the therapist instructed the parents to have the father wake him up until the next therapy session, two weeks hence.

The boy was dry during the whole two-week period. The therapist then instructed the parents to flip a coin each day to decide who would wake the boy up the next morning. Again, the boy was dry for two weeks. The parents decided to divide the week up according to the convenience of each parent, three or four days for the father and three or four days for the mother. The boy was never told who would wake him in the morning. At this point, he had been dry for a month straight. The parents promised the boy a prize if would be dry for two more months. He earned the prize.

What Happened Here?

It seems that when the boy knew his father would wake him in the morning, he was dry. When both parents woke on different nights, the boy could at least expect that his father might wake him in the morning.

But how could an event that happens the next day affect the boy the night before? This is the puzzle.

The therapist asked the parents what was different now that the boy was dry. The mother said she felt much relief that she didn't have to look forward to a wet bed in the morning. She explained further that the relief might have made her less nervous in the evening and thus more tolerant of the boy. There were fewer hassles about homework and bedtime.

So it seems that the relaxed mother led to a more relaxed boy, and thus he didn't wet his bed that night.

This is case where A (an antecedent condition) caused the problem. Removing or changing it solved the problem. But it took some good questioning by the therapist to discover it.

Fear of Flying

The fear of flying is a fairly common fear; it is estimated that 10 per cent of the population avoid flying due to this fear.

The fear of flying can be overcome with CBT treatment.

There are three important elements that patients are given during the treatment:

1) technical knowledge of flying in order to overcome unfounded fears about plane crashes
2) opportunity to learn to deal with panic anxiety on the plane
3) exposure to the stimuli in order to exercise coping mechanisms

Many people have totally unfounded fears about a plane's strength. For example, they fear air turbulence, when turbulence *never* causes crashes. Therapists can help their patients by giving them a good book on flying written for those with the fear of flying. The book *White Knuckles* has helped my patients.

Patients should be prepared to experience anxiety, particularly just before and at takeoff. They should expect it and be prepared for it. They should tell a stewardess that they have the fear; she will be more attentive to them. They should learn deep breathing relaxation in therapy and use it in the airport, waiting to board and on the plane.

They should also have a game (on his iPhone), a magazine, or a book to use for distraction purposes.

Exposure is the key to success. Some cities (New York) have airlines that treat potential passengers with exposure. They have groups of phobic people enter the plane, take a seat, and listen to the motor rev up, and then as a "graduation ceremony," they take a one-hour flight. This is done gradually and can be very helpful. Those who live in cities that don't have such an arrangement can do exposure in a different way. They take at least two trips to the airport with a suitcase, as if they were going on a flight. They enter the airport and look at the flight notices and wait with eyes closed, imagining that today they will fly. After they've done it once, the therapist can do relaxation and imaginary exposure in the clinic. There are also flight films on YouTube shot from the plane's window, which can give them a feeling somewhat of really flying. That would be their exposure. I have treated people who have overcome this fear with no more exposure than the two trips to the airport (they sent me postcards from their destination).

It can be done. Therapy should only be started once the person has reserved a seat on a flight. Two to three weeks before the flight is enough time to do the therapy.

Migraine

Migraine headaches would seem to be a problem caused by internal biological matters. If so, the question is, can CBT, a psychological treatment, reduce or eliminate migraine headaches?

The answer is yes, as the following case illustrates (from Aubuchon, Haber, and Adams, 1985, *J. Behavior Therapy & Experimental Psychiatry* 16, 26–263).

When Louise was thirteen years old, she began complaining about headaches. Over the next few years, she received inordinate parental, social, and professional attention for her headaches, including comments such as, "You poor dear, that must really hurt," "Let me hug you, maybe it will help," and "I'm so sorry your head hurts. Is there anything I can do to help?" In addition, Louise's complaints often led to her being allowed to stay home from school. At age twenty-six, Louise experienced debilitating headaches almost daily. These headaches had typical migraine characteristics: some visual effects, followed by throbbing pain over her temples, nausea, and occasional vomiting. Various treatments were tried unsuccessfully, including medication, acupuncture, chiropractic, psychotherapy, and electroconvulsive shock. Demoral injections, which she received from her physician three times a week, seemed to be of some help.

Several medical examinations failed to identify an organic basis for Louise's headaches. Behaviour therapist Peter Aubuchon thought her headaches might be a psychologically learned reaction and suggested CBT treatment.

Treatment began. All Demoral injections were stopped; her husband recorded Louise's pain behaviours (e.g., complaints, going to bed, putting cold compresses on her head). The actual headaches were not recorded. Third, Louise's parents, husband, doctors, and nurses at the clinic she visited were to completely ignore all of her pain behaviour. On the other hand, these people provided positive regard to her whenever she was acting well (e.g., exercising, doing housework). Louise signed a behavioural contract agreeing to this treatment.

Once the treatment plan was implemented, they recorded the results. Starting with an average of seven pain behaviours a week, they gradually brought it down to zero pain behaviours over the course of four months.

After four months, the pain behaviours ceased completely.

We see that the CBT treatment of simply ignoring the behavioural expressions of her migraine achieved the complete cessation of these behaviours. We also know that extinction is a slow process; in this case, it took about twelve to fifteen months before full success was achieved. She reported feeling better and began doing her normal daily activities.

When we think about this, this is a truly amazing achievement. It was achieved by correct diagnosis of the cause (attention to headache behaviour) and consistent adherence to the program. CBT translated "pain," a subjective report, into "pain behaviours," which could be monitored objectively.

Bulimia

Bulimia: Also called bulimia nervosa, this is an eating disorder characterised by episodes of secretive excessive eating (binge-eating) followed by inappropriate methods of weight control, such as self-induced vomiting (purging), abuse of laxatives and diuretics, or excessive exercise.

Overview of Treatment for Bulimia Nervosa

First-line treatment for bulimia nervosa consists of nutritional rehabilitation plus psychotherapy. Nutritional rehabilitation aims to restore a structured and consistent meal pattern that typically takes the form of three meals and two snacks per day. Cognitive behavioural therapy usually includes nutritional rehabilitation and also addresses dysfunctional thoughts and problematic behaviours that maintain the disorder. Pharmacotherapy is also efficacious and often added to the treatment regimen.

Another Approach to Treatment

I will describe a case of bulimia and its strategic treatment; while this was not CBT, it can be considered as outside-the-box thinking. We will understand why it was successful according to learning theory.

Parents of a young woman came for help for their daughter, who suffered from bulimia; compulsive binging was always followed by compulsive vomiting. The young woman herself refused to come for therapy, saying it was her parents who needed help, not her.

The woman, in her present emotional state, spent most of her time binging and vomiting. She rarely left the house. She had cut off contact with her boyfriend and all her other friends. She rarely washed and didn't brush her hair.

The Attempted Solution

The parents tried to help by locking the food away at home and not giving her money to buy food. But the girl would steal food from the supermarket, so the parents gave her money so she wouldn't steal. She was also able to find the locked food in the house.

At the first session, the therapist told the parents he believed he could help their daughter, even if she refused to see him. After complimenting them on their great efforts for their daughter and acknowledging their frustration, he said he would make a bizarre request of them. But considering all the efforts they had already made to help her, he was sure they would do what he would tell them. He then said as follows:

"From now on until next week, every morning before you go to work, I would like you, Mother, to wake up your daughter, not too early nor too late, and ask her, 'What would you like to eat and vomit today?' Write down all the foods she tells you. Go out and buy them for her. If she refuses to answer your question, then you buy what she likes and usually eats. Then set the dining room table for her with her food, with plenty of her favourite foods on the table in an attractive setting. On each dish have a note: 'Food for Mary to eat and vomit.' No one else is to eat the food, only Mary.

The parents were understandably shocked by this directive. They feared this would only make things worse. But they decided to do as the doctor ordered, since they were desperate. When they came back the next week, they reported that their daughter had protested violently when she saw the food on the table; she refused to eat it but took it and hid it in her closet. The mother, following directions, put more food on the table. The mother also reported that while the binging continued, it did seem to lessen. Seeing matters seemed to improve somewhat, he told them to continue in the same way. He told the father to remind the girl several times a day, "You may eat and vomit. The food is there for you."

The following week, they reported more progress; the binging decreased even more. The girl had protested this, saying, "Why are you telling me this?" The mother continued, "You know what she said? She said, 'You're spoiling everything. It's not like it used to be.' She used to enjoy doing it but not anymore. In fact, my daughter asked if she could come and see you, because she would like to stop completely."

Analysing the Case

We can begin to understand this case and its successful resolution by comparing it with the case above of the woman who suffered from migraine headaches.

In both cases, the problem was the attempted solution (before the psychological treatment), which was offered by the family and others. In both cases, the ineffective solution was the inordinate attention given to the problem. In the case of migraine, the people tried to improve the situation by offering help by giving attention to the sick behaviours. In the case of bulimia, the problem was the family's attempt to stop the patient from binging. Both of these approaches not only did not bring relief, they reinforced the problematic behaviour, so it didn't get better, it got worse.

If we think about it, we realise that the precipitating cause of the migraine, as well as the precipitating cause of the bulimia, are unknown. But once each problem began, soon other maintaining causes (the attention) came into play; they were more important that the original, precipitating cause. Actually, it is often the situation that the attempted solution is really the problem. We saw cases of students acting out and receiving negative attention, and it was precisely this attention that was reinforcing the problem behaviour; when the attention was stopped, the problem behaviour also stopped.

I mention this case to show how outside-the-box solutions can be found, which also follow the CBT theory. Following the clear and simple CBT theory does not absolve us of using original thinking.

Chapter 6

Introduction to Treating Children's Problems

Dealing with children's problems from a CBT viewpoint differs from other approaches.

Since CBT sees the main influence for behaviour change as coming from the outside environment, children's problems are easier to deal with, since they spend all their time in closed supervised environments (either the home or school). For this reason, CBT therapists will usually not treat children directly. They will prefer to guide parents and teachers to be effective change agents in improving children's problems. Furthermore, since the child's day is under supervision, there is a much better chance of helping them than when dealing with adults. We examine various common problems with children.

Reinforcing Behaviour that Does Not Exist

As I have said elsewhere in this book, I believe the CBT therapist should try to think outside the box. As an example of this, I present the following:

A teacher wants to help one of his most difficult students. The boy is always making trouble; the teacher cannot find any positive behaviour to reinforce.

One morning, he sees the boy and goes over to him and says, "Jackie, I owe you a dollar."

The surprised boy answers, "No, you're making a mistake. You don't owe me anything."

"Oh, I know I do; I made a note in my diary. You must have behaved well."

This goes back and forth until the teacher says, "Here, please take it. I know I'm not making a mistake."

End of story.

So what went on here? The teacher, trying to start the boy on a positive path, assumes (makes up) he has already started by doing something good. This puts the boy in an awkward position. He can't be bad today after getting a dollar for being good. So he begins to act better. It is a self-fulfilling prophecy. Now, with his new-found good behaviour, the teacher has something actual to reinforce.

In strict CBT theory, we can only reinforce behaviour that really occurs. But by thinking outside the box, the teacher created something out of nothing.

Putting an Infant to Bed

We will look at a very common problem: putting a young child to bed.

All new parents are confronted with the challenge of putting infants to bed at night. Infants usually cry when put to bed in a dark room and the parent leaves.

The graph below shows the times on two different evenings when the parents put their infant to bed. The treatment was simple: the parents put the child in his bed, left the room, and did not go back if the child was crying. This is extinction; they were attempting to extinguish the crying behaviour of their child. We see in the first attempt, the child cried forty-five minutes the first night, no times the second night, ten minutes the third night, six minutes the fourth, three and one the next two nights; after that, the baby went to sleep without crying.

About two weeks later, the baby began crying again at night. That is the second attempt at extinguishing the crying behaviour. It too was extinguished completely after seven nights.

There are several things we can learn from this study:

1) The crying will stop in a short period of time if it is completely ignored.
2) It will probably return after a short period of quiet (called "spontaneous recovery").
3) If it also is completely ignored, it will also stop in several days. Then it will not come back.

This process will repeat itself with all children. It is a law of behaviour as valid as the law of gravity.

But there are several conditions that must be met. The children should not be sick; they should not be hungry or thirsty; they should be clean after a diaper change. If these four conditions exist, the crying will stop in a short period of time, a week or less.

There are those who are concerned that the baby's cry was extinguished but the baby was probably unhappy and just gave up. This can be seen not to be the case because after extinction, babies will go to bed in a smiley, happy mood, almost as if they too were happy they weren't crying.

See the graph below (from Williams, C.D. "The elimination of tantrum behavior by extinction procedures," *J. of Abnormal and Social Psychology,* 59, 269, 1959):

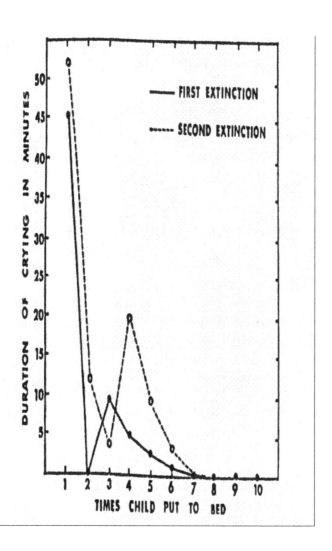

Encopresis

The next case we discuss is one of encopresis, meaning a child making a bowel movement in his pants. When a child has not achieved control by the age of five or six, this is a problem because he now goes to school, and there can be unfortunate social problems when other children become aware of this. In this case, the family was enlisted to treat the problem with the psychologist's advice.

Family Treatment of Encopresis

Kobi, six and a half years, is an intelligent and friendly boy in first grade. His parents came for help due to lack of control of his bowel movements. More specifically, he withholds for a day or two and then has a small movement in his pants. Then he refuses to go the toilet, holds back some more, and again makes in his pants. At a point when the parents realise he needs to make, they force him to go to the toilet. This cycle repeats itself over and over. As a result, the whole family is involved in Kobi's problem. There is tension, frustration, anger, with the parents accusing Kobi of not trying. They extract from him promises to do better, which of course he cannot keep.

In another session with the parents, it became clear that on rare occasions, Kobi does go to the toilet when necessary, but they could not say how often.

It is important to point out that aside from the tension this problem caused, the atmosphere in the family is a warm one; the parents have a good relationship with the children.

No medical problems were found.

Definition of the Problem Behaviour

Kobi not making in the toilet and not going to the toilet at all.

Definition of Behaviour Goal

Kobi goes to the toilet four to five times a week. The parents kept a record.

Components of the Program

- The goal was to increase his going to the toilet. We decided not to deal with the dirty pants, eve n though that disturbed the parents the most.

- They went to a homeopath to deal with his diet and help with his constipation. Because of the constipation, he had pain with the bowel movements and began to fear and avoid them. The constipation created a vicious cycle. Curing the constipation would break this cycle.

- I explained all this to the parents so they would understand that the boy didn't do this on purpose.

- I told them to give the medicine a half hour before a meal, and a half hour after the meal, they should take him to the toilet for five minutes without pressuring him to do anything. The child should be praised just for going to the toilet, even if nothing happened.

- I told them not to be angry with him if he dirtied his pants. Just to calmly change his pants without commenting.

- In my discussion with the parents, we looked for an appropriate reinforcement when he went to the toilet.

When I found it, I felt like Archimedes. Kobi has two sisters, ages eight and ten. They were very much involved with the Kobi's problem. They saw what happened every day after every event. They shared his sorrow and his happiness. I chose the sisters as change agents. I asked them to make a table on a large cardboard and mark the days of the week on it. I told them that each time Kobi made in the toilet, they were to draw a big colourful star, and then after celebrating, they would play a game with him. The sisters were happy to do this. They made the chart and hung it by Kobi's bed. All of this was done with much fun and laughter, and since it happened right after Kobi went to the toilet, it served as a powerful reinforcement.

Results

I met the parents after three more weeks; they did the observation of how many times Kobi made in the toilet, without intervening. It was amazing to see the change that came over them, even before there was any improvement. In place of being concerned and worried parents, they were different people. The problem bothered them less. They explained that keeping a record relieved them somewhat; they felt the solution was on the way. They also noticed for the first time that there were times that Kobi used the toilet. It seems the mere technical act of observing relieved tensions and created a less tense atmosphere at home. All this contributed greatly to Kobi's improvement.

In a follow-up meeting with the parents, they reported that Kobi made in his pants once in the fourth week, twice in the fifth, but no more in the sixth, seventh, or eighth weeks. This is not in the graph.

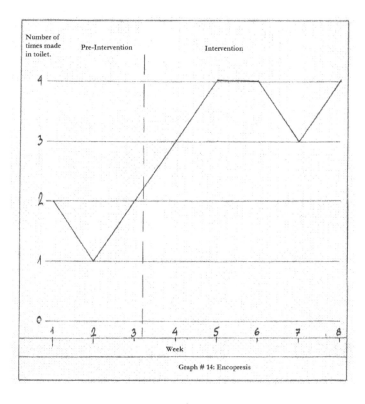

Graph # 14: Encopresis

Toilet Training in Less than a Day

Parents find ways to train their young children to urinate and defecate in the toilet. Training usually begins when the child is anywhere between two and four years old. Training can take anywhere from several weeks in the good cases to several months, sometimes more than a year, in the more difficult cases.

These differences are usually explained as being due to the child's physical maturation, which can differ from child to child.

Two CBT psychologists, Nathan Azrin and Richard Foxx, developed a clearly outlined a program for accomplishing complete toilet training in less than a day. They start when the child is two years old. Such an achievement seems to be miraculous. But in fact, it is their strict adherence to basic CBT principles that enabled them to create the program. It has been empirically tested many times and seems to be an effective program.

Below I will outline only the main elements of their program. Psychotherapists can find Azrin and Foxx's detailed program in their book, *Toilet Training in Less than a Day* (Simon and Schuster).

These are the central ideas:

- Potty training has to be pleasant experience for the child.
- Do not attempt potty training until your child is physically ready and is free of medical problems (see criterion below).
- The child has to be relaxed on the potty so that the sphincter muscles will relax and enable elimination.
- Reinforce or reward desired behaviour.
- Utilise imitation and social influence by the use of a doll that wets.

Four Signs of Child Readiness

- physiological development (bladder and bowel control)
- motor skills
- cognitive and verbal development
- emotional and social awareness
- Most two-year-olds are at this level.

Two most basic concepts:

The first concept is based on the fact that the best way to learn something is to teach it. We know that children learn from seeing, listening, and hearing. They learn action and attitudes and will copy things they have seen. So what is better than using a doll to model the appropriate potty training behaviour for your child?

They use a doll that drinks and wets. They teach children how to put the doll on the potty and how to feel their pants to see if they are wet.

Everything children do as they are guided is reinforced with sweets and sweet drinks. The whole experience is pleasant for the children, because they are showered with praise and sweets. The constant sweet drinks increase their need to urinate, so when they are placed on the potty, which is every five minutes or so, their chance of urinating is greatly increased. When that happens, they get enthusiastic verbal reinforcement and more sweets. This is the crucial moment: success and happiness at making in the potty.

The second focus is learning to feel their pants to see if they are dry or wet, as they did with the doll. If they are dry, they receive a reward; if they are wet, they get a stern look and wagging finger from their mother. This teaches them that in future, if they feel their pants, they know they should go to the potty. This combined with going to potty often and succeeding are the secrets of the success of this program.

Underlying the program is constant reinforcement, a basic element of every CBT program.

Some Examples of Outside-the-Box Thinking

I have repeatedly pointed out throughout this book that while CBT is a clear and straightforward theory, and its application to clinical cases follows directly from it, nevertheless the therapist must always be open to critical thinking and outside-the-box solutions.

What I have to say here has for the most part already been included in cases described above. I will briefly review and then add some more examples.

My idea of exposure and response repetition is a new idea not discussed in CBT literature. It comes to improve on exposure and response prevention, particularly to overcome the large dropout rate.

The unusual strategic approach of Nardone to treat cases of bulimia, which I cited above, is an example of thinking outside the box. Its success is based on learning theory.

I pointed out that the CBT approach for anger management lacks teeth, that it is weak and prone to failure. I suggested a plan to make the treatment more effective.

I offered a case for reinforcing a child who elicits little or no behaviour worthy of reinforcement. We did this by thinking outside the box, by "imagining" that the boy did some positive behaviour, which entitled him to a reinforcement. This (undeserved) reinforcement opened the path for the boy to actually engage in positive, reinforceable behaviour.

A case we did not discuss is based on the Premack principle. The Premack principle says that a less-liked behaviour can be reinforced by another more-liked behaviour when it comes right after the less-liked behaviour.

The example usually brought is when a mother says to her child, "First finish your homework (less-liked behaviour), then you can go out and play" (the more-liked behaviour).

I have a more striking example:

A woman was teaching a class of new Russian immigrants to speak English. Being all Russians, they naturally spoke among themselves in Russian. The teacher wanted to stop the Russian speaking in class. She offered a stick of chewing gum to the row of students who spoke less often in Russian. This reduced the Russian speaking throughout the class. But as she tried to thin out the reinforcement (giving it less often), the Russian speaking returned.

She then tried the Premack principle. She said, "In this class period for learning English, the students can tell us about their home life in Russia before they came to the States, and they can tell it over in Russian." The students were shocked and pleasantly surprised. "But," the teacher added, "if I give you permission to speak Russian in my English class, you must first speak English for five minutes, then the rest of the class period can be in Russian."

They readily agreed. The first week, they first spoke English for five minutes, then Russian for the remaining forty minutes. The next week, the teacher said, "That wasn't hard. This week, I want you to speak English for the first ten minutes, then for the remaining thirty-five minutes, you can speak all Russian." The following week, she upped the ante to fifteen minutes English and thirty minutes Russian. Each week, they had to speak more English while receiving less reinforcement: less time allowed for Russian speaking, since the class period was only forty-five minutes.

This is a counterintuitive result. Giving more and receiving less and being happy with the arrangement. It is counterintuitive, but it fits reinforcement theory perfectly.

The plan was created because the teacher thought outside the box.

The following case is also, in a sense, thinking outside the box. It would more reasonably be called pushing the envelope. It is a case of a nine-year-old pupil who disturbed in class incessantly. The teacher made a deal with the boy. If he did not disturb anyone for five minutes straight, he would get an X. If he earned five Xs in a period of fifty minutes, he would be allowed to play with a game he especially liked during recess.

Below we see the graph of preintervention and then intervention.

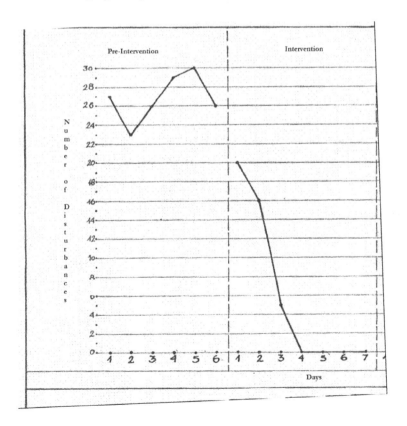

The average disruptions during baseline was twenty-seven. The first day of the intervention (receiving Xs), it went down to twenty and then to sixteen. This improvement didn't satisfy the teacher, so she changed the rules. He would receive half an X if he did not disturb for three minutes and then the other half of the X if he was again quiet for three minutes, even if he disturbed between the two three-minute periods.

Then the disturbances plummeted sharply, down to five and then to zero.

This succeeded so dramatically because the teacher reduced the challenge to three minutes, which was about the average during baseline. Remember that there were twenty-seven disturbances in a fifty-minute period, which is a disturbance about every two minutes. So by setting the challenge just a bit higher than the baseline, she practically guaranteed success.

This is a lesson all therapists should learn: set the challenge for your patients that practically assures their success.

A Final Word

I hope this book has lived up to the reader's expectations. My expectations were to enlighten and inspire the psychotherapist with the endless opportunities that exist to help your patients overcome their difficulties. When I first became acquainted with CBT about forty years ago, having come from a psychodynamic education, I saw therapy in a new light. It could be a much briefer experience for the patient while the therapist had the opportunity to gain much satisfaction with therapy's effectiveness.

A second expectation of mine was that the reader would see that CBT is not a therapy on auto-pilot. Every therapist can be innovative, can think outside the box, and can arrive at solutions not suggested by others. It is what makes our profession so challenging and so gratifying.

My personal wishes to all of you for success in helping alleviate some of the pain in our world.

Your comments are always welcome.

Drbonchek@gmail.com

Printed in the USA
CPSIA information can be obtained
at www.ICGtesting.com
LVHW041614270923
759513LV00006B/97